Connecting Cities with Macroeconomic Concerns: the Missing Link

Do local public scrvices matter?
A case study of five cities

Mila FREIRE and Mario POLÈSE,

© 2003 The International Bank for Reconstruction
and Development / The World Bank
1818 H Street NW
Washington, DC 20433
Telephone 202-473-1000
Internet: www.worldbank.org
E-mail: feedback@worldbank.org

This publication is the result of a collaborative effort of the World Bank and five partner institutions, under the direction of the World Bank and the center Urbanisation, Culture et Société of the Institut national de la recherche scientifique (INRS-UCS), in Montreal, Canada.

Mila Freire is Sector Manager for Urban Development in the Latin America and the Caribbean Region at the World Bank. Mario Polèse is Professor of Urban Economics at INRS-UCS. Pamela Echeverria is a PhD candidate at INRS-UCS.

Rights and Permissions

The cover illustration was created by Raymond Lafontaine.
The graphic design of the cover pages was made by Bertuch, l'agence graphique.

Library of Congress Cataloging-in-Publication data has been applied for.

ISBN 0-8213-5673-9

Printed and bound in Canada

Background studies available on the Web

Readers interested in a more detailed picture and analysis of each of the Southern cities covered in this study can access the background studies via Internet.

Detailed city studies were prepared by each of the city research teams. The studies for Puebla and San José are available in Spanish only. The studies for San Salvador and Belo Horizonte are also available in English and, for the latter, in Portuguese. The full titles with authors are listed below, as well as the address of the website where they can be accessed.

San José

Importancia de los bienes públicos locales para la industria alimenticia y textil: el caso de San José Costa Rica.
Author: Rosendo Pujol

Belo Horizonte

Investigación de campo de Belo Horizonte-Brasil. Industria del vestuario-segmento productivo de confecciones. Informe final.
Field Study in Belo Horizonte-Brazil. Clothing Industry-Garment Sector. Final Report.
Pesquisa de campo de Belo Horizonte-Brasil. Indústria do vestuario-segmento productivo de confecções. Relatório final.
Author: Alvaro Ramalho

San Salvador

Servicios urbanos deficientes en San Salvador: ¿Un obstaculo para la instalación de nuevas empresas?
Are Deficient Urban Services in the San Salvador Metropolitan Area Obstacles to New Businesses Development?
Authors: Mario Lungo and Ada Abrego

Puebla

Servicios públicos, infraestructura y marco regulador en el costo de las empresas del vestido y alimentos. El caso de la ciudad de Puebla (México).
Authors : Salvador Pérez-Mendoza and Fabiola Aguilar Cruz

The studies can be accessed via the virtual library of the Montreal Interuniversity Group Villes et développement at the following address:
http://gim.inrs-ucs.uquebec.ca/publicat/pub_an.html

Table of Contents

LIST OF FIGURES

LIST OF TABLES

Acknowledgments

This manuscript is the product of a research initiative launched in 2001 by a group of practioners and academics interested in examining the ways in which cities affect productivity and economic performance. Most group members began their work two years earlier during the preparation of the WBI courses on Urban and City Management. Given in partnership with the WBI and several universities, these courses were offered in Montreal, Toronto, Belo Horizonte, El Salvador, and several other capital cities around the world.

During the process of putting together the research proposal, successive surveys, discussion groups, and the final compilation of hundreds of responses, we benefited from the help and hard work of a large team of colleagues and the support of several organizations and individuals. At the risk of omitting some, we mention several of those who have contributed to this project.

First, we acknowledge our gratitude to our sponsors: the Bank-Netherlands Partnership Program, the World Bank—notably the Urban Sector Board and the Latin America and Caribbean Region—, as well as the center Urbanisation, Culture et Société of the Institut national de la recherche scientifique (INRS-UCS).

Second, we wish to recognize the coordinators of the city teams, who promoted the agenda of their own city, who did not give in to the great skepticism expressed by respondents, but persisted with great scientific nobility. The coordinators are: Rosendo Pujol, Director of ProDus (Programa de Investigación en Desarrollo Urbano Sostenible), University of Costa Rica; Salvador Pérez-Mendoza, Professor, Department of Economics, Universidad Autónoma de Puebla, Mexico; Mario Lungo, Director of Research, OPAMSS (Oficina de Planificación de la Aréa Metropolitana de San Salvador, El Salvador; Alvaro Ramalho Junior, Professor at Fundação João Pinheiro, Belo Horizonte, Brazil. They accepted the challenge of collaborating on an international project, adapting to their local context the questions and dilemmas found in other cities, with the aim of finding common threads and possible similar solutions.

Third, we would like to thank the students, too numerous to mention, who, in each city, participated in the surveys and in other aspects of the study.

Fourth, we wish to thank our colleagues for their collaboration on the work's methodological aspects, on the preparation of focus groups, on the database construction, and on the econometric analysis. Pamela Echeverria, PhD student at INRS-UCS, was central in the design of the survey and instrumental throughout the course of the study. We thank André Lemelin, Professor at INRS-UCS, who acted as our general advisor on methodological issues. Fifth, we are grateful to Pierre Frisko, liaison officer at INRS-UCS, for his assistance and excellent editing work.

Finally we wish to thank our colleagues at the World Bank, notably Danny Leipziger, John Flora, Christine Kessides, Lomil Lak, and Ofelia Haase, whose contributions greatly improved the focus and empirical relevance of this work.

Mila Freire (World Bank)   Mario Polèse (INRS-UCS)

Introduction

Urban growth is, in all parts of the world, inevitable and welcomed. Despite concerns that local governments will not be able to address those issues associated with increased urban population, the number of people living in urban centers will surpass those of the rural population by 2030. Since productivity levels are consistently higher in urban areas than in rural settings, this would seem a reason to rejoice since it suggests more people with higher salaries, better standards of living, and less poverty. But will this be the reality, or will the nightmare of hopeless poverty overshadow the positive feelings of economic wealth and progress?

This disjunction between the wonders of the city and the horrors facing the homeless poor is at the core of any professional work on economic development and urban management issues. On one hand, everyone agrees that cities are wonderful instruments of change, culture, motivation and progress. Cities are also at the core of democratic progress. Local government elections offer a laboratory in which citizens can exercise their rights to political action. The importance of cities throughout human civilization is well demonstrated by the protection they enjoyed during humanity's most violent periods, and this often at the expense of the rural sector.

On the other hand, cities are often unable to adequately answer to the needs of newcomers. Deficits in housing, water and sanitation have an immediate impact on environmental degradation, health indicators, child mortality, and the self-esteem of city inhabitants. City managers and mayors must deal with this disjunction, and make decisions without adequate resources. They face challenges that range from shrewdly handling municipal finances, to providing extended services in an effort to reach the poor.

Latin American cities are at the centre of three powerful trends: urbanization, globalization and decentralization. The associated risks and opportunities will shape the future of the region. Urbanization will continue to reach rates of 80-85%, which are characteristic of mature cities. At the same time, globalization, which heightens competition among cities for market shares and jobs in East Asia, is gradually also reaching the Latin American cities of Brazil and Argentina. Cities that are unable to respond to the challenges of new technology and of an ever-increasing demand for knowledge seem to be fated to lag behind. Decentralization, which forces cities to take on greater responsibility for their own management and revenues, provides both an opportunity and a challenge as a response to urbanization and globalization.

At present, cities are taking on roles that extend far beyond the traditional provision of infrastructure and services. A paradigm shift may be detected. Cities are seeing themselves as engines of economic growth, providers and managers of land, and suppliers of social services, such as education and health. They rightly understand their role as facilitating or, in economic jargon, taking care of the investment climate and the externalities that impact decisions of investment and production.

The role of the cities in promoting employment and growth has been recognized by many cities. European and Chinese cities are moving to create investor-friendly environments, eliminating red tape, and increasing employment opportunities. They are supporting the informal economy and promoting micro-credit schemes. In the recent past, the Bank and its clients have recognized the role of cities in promoting development and alleviating poverty. The urban strategy proposed by the Bank in 2000 is very direct. It promotes

a) a national urban policy that includes a general framework establishing guidelines on the powers and responsibilities of cities;

b) participatory city development strategies, and the development of each community's relative advantages;

c) a focus on urban poverty and upgrading; and

d) technical assistance and institutional strengthening at all levels of the public sector and private constituencies to understand the dynamics of cities and how to best use their energies.

In this framework, some issues appear more pressing than others. Globalization seems the most urgent. Trends of increased trade and capital movement bring with them increasing flows of people, goods, capital, services and ideas. Some cities have acquired a new preeminence because of the special functions they perform in the new global economy, with its emphasis on human capital, information technology, and flexible administrative systems.

The world today is not only more urbanized; it is obviously richer than it was fifty years ago. Between 1950-1992, per capita income more than tripled. The flow of private investment to developing countries increased from US$5 billion to nearly US$160 billion between 1970 and 1993. The rapid integration of economies stems from a convergence of three major trends: (a) the drop in commodity prices; (b) the ascendancy of transnational capitals; and (c) new technologies. The latter trend has also had an impact in other fields, e.g. new technologies in the material sciences and in biotechnology have facilitated new production processes, revolutionized business transactions, and encouraged creativity.

In a global world, the network of cities changes and evolves. It is clear that cities are increasingly linked in interdependent ways, some cities assuming key functions in the global systems of finance, transportation, telecommunications and services (the so-called world cities or global cities). Having long been engines of growth and leaders in the creation of national wealth, cities now occupy a special place in the global era. Many cities account for a considerable proportion of their nation's GDP.

Under the forces of globalization, there is a certain convergence of cities from various parts of the world and at different stages of economic development. Four commonalities appear to characterize globalized cities (Cohen, 1996). First, urban unemployment remains high, reaching 15% in France, 22% in Spain, 10.6% in Buenos Aires and 7.2% in metropolitan Lagos. Second, urban infrastructure suffers from inadequate maintenance in developed countries, such as the failed water and sewage systems in Chicago and Washington, and the electricity blackouts of the Eastern Seaboard. In developing countries, lack or inadequacy of investment in infrastructure has led to widespread problems in the provision of water supply, urban sanitation and transportation. Fourth, rising social conflict is an emergent problem in cities, resulting, in part, from keener competition for jobs, and from a freer flow of people between countries. Globalization has also generated international flows of labour and all types of migrants in recent decades. In the cities of industrialized countries, new immigrants and minority groups have generated new political and social pressures on the urban scene. In the cities of developing countries, such as in Rio de Janeiro, Medellin and Lima, urban crime has become a political issue (Gilbert, 1996).

Indeed, globalization has not benefited all cities. The truth is that, while globalization has brought about new opportunities and created wealth for some cities, it has, at the same time, severely marginalized others. The marginalized city may occur in any part of the world, if it remains outside the flow of cyber-activity due to inadequate information infrastructure, or an inability to plug itself into the new global economy.

The same fate may be observed, in subtler ways, in cities where inefficient forms of governance hinder the normal development of business along a path of comparative advantage. The most common factor contributing to this is corruption in local government. Corruption distorts resource allocation and production decisions, and often brings with it misinformation, lack of transparency, lack of security, violence, and, finally, a failure by the local government to provide local public goods, e.g. water, solid waste, lighting, power, etc., within acceptable conditions.

This work encompasses the story of five research centers, thousands of surveys sent and not returned, and several hundreds of firms who shared with us their concerns. The picture it paints is very simple. In four countries and hundreds of business firms we found the same (i) lack of trust in authority and skepticism that any good could ever come from local government interventions; (ii) phenomenal capacity to persist with business ventures, even when these were victims of crime half the time, and when more than 10% of net revenues are spend on security; and (iii) resignation to the fact that each citizen must take care of their own problems.

It also shows that if some of the most problematic public services were better provided, Latin cities could produce more and better, employ higher paid labour, expand production, be able to abide by export contracts, and generate more employment.

It will take some time until the cities of the South find the same comfort, in terms of security and public goods, that Montreal displays in this sample. While cities are hardly comparable, examining their core is a fascinating business, not so much because of the differences we find, but because of the striking similarities between their firms and people, regardless of latitude or dominant culture.

CHAPTER 1

Cities, Agglomeration Economies, Local Public Services and Economic Growth: a Reappraisal

The purpose of this chapter is to set the stage for the empirical chapters to follow. The chapter is divided into two parts. We begin with a review of the state of knowledge on the relationship between urban areas (cities) and national economic growth, and proceed to focus on so-called localized public services, examining the role of institutions and the public sector in explaining the contribution of cities to national economic growth.

1. CITIES AND ECONOMIC GROWTH

The link between cities and economic growth, defined as a long-term sustained increase in real per capita incomes or product[1], is both clear and unclear. The link is clear because the positive relationship between urbanization (and to some extent, city size) and per capita incomes is undeniable. It is not surprising that cities are sometimes described as "engines of growth," to use an established expression. The positive link is indeed irrefutable. However, there is some debate on the direction of causation, i.e., whether growth brings urbanization or whether urbanization per se causes economic growth. Some of this debate stems from the sometimes-ambiguous use of the word "city," which can have both a political meaning and a concept of urban agglomeration. The first part reviews the literature on the link between cities and economic growth, beginning with the positive link and the "engine of growth" hypotheses.

The Positive Link

The evidence of a positive link between cities (urban areas) and economic development is overwhelming. An abundant literature has accumulated demonstrating the positive relationship between urban areas (specifically, their share of national populations) and national economic growth. Numerous studies have, time and again, confirmed the positive relationship between per capita income and urbanization levels (Fay and Opal, 2000; Jones and Koné, 1996; Lemelin and Polèse, 1995; Tolley and Thomas, 1987). Other studies have repeatedly demonstrated the disproportionate contribution of urban areas to national income and product (Ciccolla, 1999; Prud'homme, 1997; Peterson, 1991; World Bank, 1991). Others again have demonstrated the positive link between productivity and the agglomeration of economic activity in cities (Ciccone and Hall, 1996; Glaeser, 1998; Henderson, 1988; Krugman, 1991; Rauch, 1993; Quigley, 1998).

The basic evidence is summarized in Figures 1.1 and 1.2, and in Table 1.1. Thus, greater Mexico City, with approximately 15% of the national population, generated some 34% of GNP. In El Salvador, greater San Salvador accounted for 26% of population, but generated 44% of GNP. For all cities, the contribution of urban areas to GNP is greater than their share of the national population (all ratios are above 1.0—see last column). And in all cases the contribution of larger urban centres is proportionally greater. Thus, the ratio for Mexico City is higher than that for all Mexican cities. In sum, cities, especially bigger cities, mean higher productivity and higher per capita incomes. The results in Table 1.1 remain consistent for nations with different economic systems and histories (note the results for Russia and China), and therefore cannot simply be explained by what some would call the unequal development patterns of (capitalist) free market economies. Manifestly, there is something in the very nature of urban agglomerations that contributes positively to higher incomes.

Table 1.1: The Economic Importance of Cities*

Urban Area	Country	(A) Population	(B) GNP	Ratio
		Percentage of National Total		
		(%)	(%)	B/A
Sao Paulo	Brazil	8.6	36.1	4.20
Buenos Aires	Argentina	35.0	53.0	1.51
Santiago de Chile	Chile	35.6	47.4	1.33
Lima	Peru	28.1	43.1	1.53
Guayaquil	Ecuador	13.1	30.1	2.30
Mexico	Mexico	14.2	33.6	2.37
All Cities	Mexico	60.1	79.7	1.33
San Salvador	El Salvador	25.8	44.1	1.71
Port-au-Prince	Haiti	15.1	38.7	2.56
All Cities	Haiti	24.2	57.6	2.38
Casablanca	Morocco	12.1	25.1	2.07
Abidjan	Ivory Coast	18.1	33.1	1.83
Nairobi	Kenya	5.2	20.1	3.87
All Cities	Kenya	11.9	30.3	2.55
Karachi	Pakistan	6.1	16.1	2.64
All Cities	India	19.9	38.9	1.95
Shanghai	China	1.2	12.5	10.42
Manila	Philippines	12.1	25.1	2.07
Bangkok	Thailand	10.9	37.4	3.43
Moscow	Russia	5.8	10.9	1.88
All Cities	Turkey	47.1	70.1	1.49

* Results are for years within the range 1975-1995, depending on the case.
Sources: World Bank, 1991; Ciccolla, 1999; De Mattos, 1999; Economist, 1997; PRISMA, 1996; Prud'homme, 1997.

The concept of "agglomeration economies," familiar to geographers and economists, is often used to explain the higher productivity of (non-agricultural) firms in urban settings. The concept goes back to the early writings on industrial location (Isard, 1956; Hoover, 1948; Weber, 1909), and is now a standard element in urban and regional economics[2]. In simple terms, agglomeration economies refer to the productivity gains derived from the geographic clustering of firms and people; see for example Henderson (1988) for an econometric application to Brazilian and U.S. cities. For a particular firm, the gains derived from being located in an urban area can have various sources: scale economies due to greater market size (within close range); lower infrastructure costs (spread over a greater number of users); lower information and transaction costs because of the greater range and facility of face-to-face contacts; more flexible and rapid input relationships, given the greater diversity (and proximity) of potential suppliers; lower training and recruitment costs due to the presence of a large and diversified labour pool which, in turn, has a direct impact on labour productivity. Agglomeration economies are very heterogeneous, and their precise mix and importance will be different for different firms and for different urban areas[3]. Table 1.1 suggests that such "economies" indeed exist, but it does not tell us what, exactly, lies behind them in each case. In the early 1990's, a World Bank study introduced the notion of "urban productivity" to cover the broad range of factors that make cities more productive (World Bank, 1991). This goes beyond the traditional definition of agglomeration economies to also include institutional factors, a point to which we shall return.

Figure 1.1: GNP Per Capita and Urbanization Levels

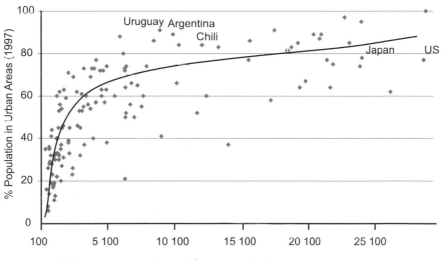

GNP per capita (1997) in US$ adjusted for differences in purchasing power
(each dot represents a nation)

There is little evidence that agglomeration economies are less important today than in the past. Indeed, the evidence suggests that the significance of agglomeration economies is growing, sparking ever greater geographic concentrations of economic activity, as a result of both the impact of new information technologies, and the gradual shift in national economic structures towards more knowledge-intensive sectors (Gasper and Glaeser, 1998; Glaeser, 1998; Quigley, 1998; Polèse and Shearmur, 2003). From a historical perspective, agglomeration may also be viewed as a necessary corollary of the development of functioning market economies. Cities allow goods, ideas, and people to come together for purposes of exchange and production. This, in turn, allows society to reap the gains from trade and specialization. It is difficult to imagine a modern market economy without markets, i.e., market places. Indeed, it can be argued that this is the (economic) essence of the city. Cities and towns arose as market centers, centers of distribution, import-export and finance, long before the advent of the modern industrial era.

Figure 1.2: GNP Per Capita and Urbanization Levels

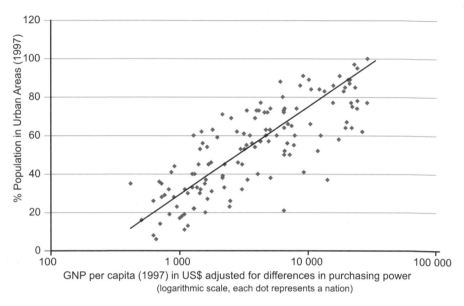

GNP per capita (1997) in US$ adjusted for differences in purchasing power
(logarithmic scale, each dot represents a nation)

Rosenthal and Strange (2001), seeking the microeconomic foundations of agglomeration, emphasize three elements: knowledge spillovers, labour market pooling, and input sharing. These foundations are not independent of public policy or local institutional context. They implicitly assume the ability of cities to provide an environment where: 1) economic agents can meet and communicate easily (knowledge spillovers); 2) labour moves unencumbered within the urban area (labour market pooling); 3) public infrastructure is adequately provided and goods are efficiently transported (input sharing). We shall argue that such a local institutional context cannot be universally assumed. This, in turn, affects the potential gains that may be reaped from agglomeration, and thus also the potential of cities to act as engines of economic growth.

Cities as Engines of Economic Growth?

There exists a long tradition of scholarship interested in the role of cities in history, and as fountainheads of "civilization" (however defined), social transformation and, ultimately, economic growth (the classic works of Pirenne (1925) on the medieval city and, more recently, Bairoch (1988) and Hall (1999)). Jacobs (1969, 1984) argues that cities are the prime movers in national economic growth, the essential medium by which ideas circulate and innovation occurs: interaction among people in cities promotes innovation and raises productivity. This is at the root of the more recent concept of "knowledge spillovers." The evidence is strong, at least for industrialized nations[4], that knowledge spillovers exist and, as a corollary, that innovation is sensitive to agglomeration (Gleaser et al., 1992; Duranton and Puga, 2002). Thus, Gleaser et al. (1992) introduce the idea of "dynamic externalities" to define the possible growth impact of agglomeration. However, quoting Gleaser et al. (1992: 1126-1127), "knowledge spillovers are particularly effective in cities where communication between people is most extensive... If (author's emphasis) proximity facilitates the transmission of ideas, then we should expect knowledge spillovers to be important." This brings to mind our earlier caveat on the local institutional context.

The argument that agglomeration (at least, beyond the village level) produces behavioral and cultural change appears irrefutable. These changes are the focus in much of urban sociology and anthropology: changing family structures, declining birth rates, reduced religious practice, etc. The old German adage, harking back to medieval times, "Stadtluft macht Frei" (City air makes you free) nicely captures the perceived liberating influence of city life. It is difficult to argue with the observation that, since the beginning of recorded history, cities have been centers of artistic creation, drawing in the talented and creative minds of their times: Athens, Venice, Vienna, and Paris are obvious examples. In more recent times, an abundance of literature has added to the writings on knowledge spillovers, by demonstrating that innovation and technologically advanced activities are sensitive to agglomeration (Audertsch and Feldman, 1996; Braczyk et al., 1998; Hall, 2000; Maillat, 1998). Using U.S. and French data, Dumais et al. (1997) and Duranton and Puga (2002), also observe a positive relationship between business startup (plant openings) and agglomeration.

In sum, the evidence that cities (thus also urbanization, at least beyond some minimum threshold) are necessary conditions for innovation, social change, and economic growth is very strong. Equally, the evidence that cities, as vehicles facilitating interaction and the concentration of talent, are necessary for innovation and technological progress appears irrefutable. When added to the positive relationship between income levels, city size, and urbanization (as shown in Figures 1.1 and 1.2, and Table 1.1), the inference that cities will act as engines of growth appears entirely reasonable. However, the evidence that cities (or urbanization) actually cause economic growth is less convincing. The growth effect, if any, is probably small, and very sensitive to national and local institutional contexts, as well as, specifically, to what we shall call "localized public services."

Cities: Places or Actors?

Krugman (1996) draws an essential distinction between cities or urban areas as policy-making units and cities as places for production and exchange: the attributes of place (among which the size of the urban area) will affect the productivity of firms and thus, indirectly, the level of national income. The evidence in Table 1.1 refers to urban areas or, more accurately, in the vocabulary of statistical agencies, to urban agglomerations, defined generally as (urban) settlements above some minimal population or density threshold[5], where the geographic boundary of agglomerations normally corresponds to the outer limits of their commuting sheds. The concept of "agglomeration economies" refers, by definition, to urban agglomerations (to places), but need not necessarily correspond to administrative or political units. Indeed, only in rare cases do urban agglomerations correspond to political units, regardless of their national nomenclature (municipalities, cities, communes, cantons, etc). However, in most languages (at least in English, French and Spanish), the word "city" has both meanings. It can refer to both a political-administrative unit, as in the City of Paris, and, in its generic usage, to an urban area. A resident of the suburbs of Paris, if asked, "What city are you from?" may well answer Paris, even if he or she lives beyond the administrative boundaries of the City of Paris.

The double meaning of "city" is the source of much confusion. In the German adage quoted earlier, referring to the historically liberating effects of cities, the word "city" is implicitly used to designate both a generic entity (an urban place) and an administrative-political unit. This use is valid in its historical context. In the Middle Ages and the Renaissance, "cities" (i.e., urban places) in Germany, Italy and other parts of Western Europe often had separate charters, creating distinct institutional environments, which facilitated trade and economic activity. Cities were organized as independent corporations with, in essence, their own constitutions[6]. By contrast, Russia, at that time, had no Western-model corporate towns, no municipal law, and no maxims such as "City air makes you free" (Heer, 1962:100). This may explain, in part, why Russia was later less successful in promoting economic growth.

The point is this: it is only valid to use the two meanings interchangeably where the term "cities" (i.e., urban areas) refers to distinct institutional environments that, in turn, significantly impact economic behaviour. This is not the case in most nations today. While there are exceptions, such as the city-state of Singapore and several of the emerging mega-urban areas of East Asia (Jakarta, Hong-Kong and Pearl River in China), the role of "cities" (political-administrative definition) in most nations is mainly to deliver local public services. While local legislation and administrative regulations are key factors in determining the investment climate and competitiveness of a given region, most of the legal-institutional environment remains the fora of national legislation, or state/provincial legislation in federations.

A Word of Caution

The proposition that agglomeration, as such, stimulates growth remains popular among policymakers (and academics). The possibility of stimulating growth through changes in the spatial allocation of resources promises a comparatively easy path to development, certainly easier than institutional change. The idea that agglomeration, as such, promotes growth has, in various periods, given rise to economic development strategies. While accepted at the time, these strategies fell out of favor as their limits became apparent. Parr (1999a, b) provides an excellent analysis of the rise and fall of growth-pole strategies, another casualty in the long list of models in search of a panacea. Industrial complexes (Isard, 1959), a popular concept during the 1950s and 1960s, have also come and gone.

Yet, the notion that growth can be deliberately jump-started by steering the location of industry keeps reappearing. Currently, "growth clusters" (see Porter 1996, 2000) once again promise that fostering the concentration of related industries can stimulate sustained growth. While it is certainly true that creating a favorable environment that allows firms to interact is a positive factor, the fundaments of infrastructure, including industrial parks, are essential preconditions for growth (more on this later). However, causality may work in the other direction. Firms may cluster because they perceive it to be in their interest, responding to market (and public policy) signals, and hopefully sparking clusters that translate into agglomeration economics for the firms concerned. However it is debatable if agglomeration, as such (or "clustering"), will in turn trigger a sustained period of innovation, creativity, and economic growth. As Hall (2000) admits, the conditions that make a particular city "creative" at a given moment in history are perhaps not amenable to a universal theory.

The question then arises: why is agglomeration not sufficient to trigger growth, and why do the gains from agglomeration emerge more readily in some places than others? The gains may perhaps materialize, but only under specific conditions. Arguably, cities can also become obstacles to growth to the extent that urbanization (agglomeration) is a necessary complement of growth (an essential adjustment), and that the efficient management of cities requires a combination of institutions and localized public services that some societies, more than others, find it difficult to provide. In this context, since agglomeration economies are sensitive to institutions, culture, and national histories, then the economic consequences of urbanization will also vary according to the same factors.

2. INSTITUTIONS, LOCALIZED PUBLIC SERVICES AND ECONOMIC GROWTH

In the sections that follow, we shall explore the links between the public sector and agglomeration. We specifically look at the role of "localized" public services, that is, services that are necessarily tied to place. The externalities that underlie agglomeration economies are, we shall argue, very sensitive to institutions and localized public services.

What Sets the Upper Limits of Agglomeration Economies?

At any given moment in time, the "pure" gains from agglomeration, i.e., due to the more efficient geographic allocation of resources, are essentially limited by prevailing technological conditions. Beyond that, we suggest it is largely the public sector that sets the upper limits on the gains from agglomeration and, thus, also from urbanization. Admittedly, what Olson (2000: 175) calls spontaneous markets will arise in cities in the absence of a functioning public sector and adequate institutions. The vitality of the informal sector in many cities of the developing world bears witness to this. However, these are limited markets where the costs, both financial and economic, of doing business are high, partly because of the absence (or deficiency) of a wide range of public goods: contract enforcement mechanisms, property rights, public safety, etc.

The ability to "productively" interact is a core attribute of agglomeration economies: implicit is the presence of urban places where people can securely and comfortably congregate to trade, communicate, and work. Agglomeration economies will be maximized where these conditions are present. Some hundred years ago, before the concept was coined, Howe (1915: 4) observed: "The city can only live by co-operation; by co-operation in a million unseen ways. Without co-operation for a single day a great city would stand still." Howe (1915) then goes on to describe the myriad new public services needed to make a "modern" city work. The term "civic culture" springs to mind. In sum, urbanization, if its economic benefits are to be fully reaped, requires fundamental institutional and perhaps also cultural changes for which some societies are initially better prepared than others.

Unraveling the relative impact of public policies and institutions (national, regional, local) is almost impossible; the relative weight of specific public policies will vary from one case to another. There is little doubt that national macroeconomic policies, institutions, history, and culture are determining factors in the relative levels of economic development of nations and peoples and, thus, indirectly, of the economic potential of their cities. Fukuyama (1995), Landis (1998), and OECD (2001) stress the role of culture and values, while Acemoglu et al. (2001), and Easterly and Levine (2002) emphasize institutions. The Argentinean case, cited above, is undoubtedly an example, at least in part, of faulty institutions. In sum, the productivity of cities (to use the term coined by the World Bank, 1991) is necessarily a function of national conditions and institutions. Without sound macroeconomic policies, without the adequate provision of basic education and health services, and without an appropriate national institutional framework, the potential benefits to be reaped from agglomeration will necessarily be lower. The converse may also be true. If local governments are afflicted with corruption and inefficiency, the local economy will suffer, and the consequences of this will spread to the surrounding area.

Localized Public Services

How important then are local policies and local public services? The answer is not a simple one, especially because the dividing line between what is local, regional, and national varies from one nation to another. Water may be a national responsibility in one nation (whether privately or publicly provided), but a municipal one in another. Legislation at the national level (or state level in federations) will largely define the political-administrative structures by which cities are governed. In most nations, local levels of government or administration (municipalities, towns, special purpose agencies, etc.) are creations of senior levels of government. Policies affecting transportation (petrol taxation, highway construction, etc.) will often be decided at the state or national level. Locally-provided services can include road maintenance, public transit, sanitation, refuse collection, public order, and regulatory matters (permits, zoning, etc.), to name only a few.

We have thus chosen to use the term "localized" public services, without reference to the level of government or type of agency mandated to deliver them. In many cases, local public service provision will involve more than one level of government. For example, ensuring the fluid movement of vehicles in the city might involve the municipal government (traffic control), the regional government (road construction and maintenance) and the national government (vehicle licensing and taxation). The essential point is this: from the point of view of the firm and other users, localized public services and infrastructure are, by definition, tied to place. A local firm (say, in the apparel industry) cannot chose to import better roads, public security, or sewage systems from elsewhere. The full cost of inferior services and infrastructure will necessarily be borne by the firm. If the firm's potential customers are international, then higher costs may mean the loss of markets, the cessation of production, or even that production will never have taken place. These impacts are, by definition, difficult to measure, but no less real. The quality of localized public services and institutions can, we suggest, have an impact on productivity and levels of production.

We may safely argue that the higher the national level of urbanization, the greater will be the negative effect on the GDP of poor institutions and inferior localized public services: Fay and Opal (2000) speak of dysfunctional cities. We have equally coined the term "urban failure" to designate situations where urban firms cannot generate sufficient production and employment to significantly reduce urban poverty (Polèse, 1998c), that is, urban places where the production costs faced by firms are such that production will be lower (or simply not take place), specifically because of the high costs of localized public services. We have divided localized public services into two classes: 1) "hard" services, basically infrastructure; and 2) "soft" services, emphasizing "pure" public goods that cannot be readily provided through private means. The local institutional environment (norms, regulations, legal order, etc.) would fall in the second class. The distinction matters because, in the case of pure localized public goods, the firm (or other user) is entirely at the mercy of the public sector to provide the service. Not only is the service tied to place, but there is also no alternative to public provision. The firm is doubly captive. We shall however first look at "hard" localized public services, which in most cases are amenable to privatization or self-provision.

Hard (privatizable) Localized Public Services

Numerous studies have, time and again, demonstrated the positive link between economic performance and the quality and quantity of public infrastructure: power, water and sanitation, roads and highways, harbors and airports, telecommunications, etc. (Arsen, 1997; Aschauer, 1993, 2000; Bidder and Smith, 1996; Crihfield and McGuire, 1997; Eberts, 1991; Hakfoort, 1996; Kessides, 1992, 1996; Lobo and Rantisi, 1999; Morrison and Schwartz, 1992; Munnell, 1992; Nadiri and Manuens, 1991; Wang, 2002). Many of these studies deal with the U.S. economy and the links between infrastructure investment (often in a specific infrastructure) and productivity in the manufacturing sector. A detailed discussion of the various methodologies or specific findings in each analysis falls beyond the purview of our study. We can,

however, safely state that, today, the positive link between productivity and investments in infrastructure is well-established, although precise estimates (for example,
of the impact of an investment of x dollars in infrastructure y on GDP growth in
period t) remain difficult and will necessarily vary according to the particular
characteristics (region, time, infrastructure) of the case examined.

That being said, let us return to the link between public policy and agglomeration
economies. Most of the infrastructure assets listed above are "privatizable" since
users can be directly charged, with the notable exception of free-access highways
and roads (and most roads fall into this category). The private sector will "normally"
provide water and power, for example, if the demand exists. The public sector
enters into the picture because some types of infrastructure are, at least in part,
natural monopolies (especially those with network characteristics, such as power
transmission), or entail important social and economic externalities (notably water
and sanitation) and, as such, require an adequate regulatory environment to function
properly. All this is well known. In many cases, such types of infrastructure will be
publicly provided, as is the case for water in most U.S. and Canadian municipalities.
The range of public-private arrangements is almost limitless (concessions, BOT,
etc.), and is well documented; see for example Blaicklock (1994) and World Bank
(1994).

Thus, although in principle many types of infrastructure can be provided by the
private sector, cases of inadequate infrastructure provision will most often have their
origin in a weak or malfunctioning public sector. The link with macroeconomics is
most evident in cases where infrastructure is provided and financed by the public
sector; i.e., where the debts and other financial commitments of the infrastructure
provider spill over into the national treasury (and vice-versa). In many developing
nations, especially those most indebted, this remains one of the chief factors
driving the push to privatization. But, we then confront the apparent paradox that,
to succeed, privatization, a seeming weakening of the state, requires a strong (and
honest) public sector, capable of providing the necessary regulatory environment.
Infrastructure investment in developing nations is highly dependant on the existence
of a favorable macroeconomic and institutional climate. As Kessides (1996) wisely
cautions, infrastructure investment alone will ensure neither higher productivity
nor growth, if not complemented by other conditions. Again, prudence is in order
when inferring causality. The observed positive link between infrastructure and
economic performance (as demonstrated in the studies cited at the outset of this
section) often implicitly subsumes conditions that are not necessarily universally
present. A full discussion of the issues falls beyond the scope of this study. Suffice
it to say that the link between an effective public sector and adequate infrastructure
provision is a strong one, which brings us back to agglomeration economies.

The link between infrastructure and agglomeration economies is not difficult
to comprehend, although few authors explicitly make the connection in the context
of developing nations. If an urban place suffers from continued power blackouts
and water shortages, productivity will necessarily decrease, brining down the
upper limit of potential of agglomeration economies. Lall, Shalizi and Deichmann
(2001), in their study of India, emphasize the link with interurban transportation
networks[7]. A growing literature examines the impact of inferior infrastructure

on productivity and economic performance in developing nations (Anas and Lee, 1988; Baumol and Lee, 1991; Bjorvatn, 2000; Lee, 1988, 1989, 1992; Lee, Anas and Oh, 1999; Lee, Anas, Verma and Murray, 1996; Reinikka and Svensson, 1999). The link with cities and agglomeration economies is largely implicit since most of the infrastructure studied is, almost by definition, necessary for the functioning of efficient urban places. Bjorvatn (2000) argues that the poor quality of infrastructure in many developing nations is a major factor in explaining the disappointing level of investment in the manufacturing sector, which is necessarily located in cities or in peri-urban areas. In sum, the low productivity of urban places (or its corollary, the low rate of return on private investment in manufacturing) can, in part, be traced back to infrastructure deficiencies.

The Private Costs of Inferior Infrastructure

The numerous studies by Lee and his colleagues (see previous citations) provide by far the richest information to date on the impact of public infrastructure deficiencies on the production costs of manufacturing establishments. The most recent paper (Lee, Anas and Oh, 1999) compares results for Nigeria, Indonesia, and Thailand, drawing on an extensive survey of manufacturing establishments. Lee and his colleagues observe that the private costs, i.e., those borne by manufacturing establishments, of deficiencies in infrastructure can be substantial, and that the burdens are much greater for smaller establishments than for their larger counterparts, essentially because smaller establishments cannot afford private supply (a point to which we shall return). Like Wang (2002) and World Bank (1991), Lee and his colleagues identify infrastructure as "intermediate inputs" in the production process. Where these inputs are missing or too costly, production may simply not take place. It is not difficult to infer the negative implications for both the birth and expansion of firms, for income and employment creation, and ultimately, poverty reduction.

The negative impacts of infrastructure deficiencies on production costs can take various forms. In the case of power, it can translate into production hours lost due to power failures or interruptions (approximately 7% of lost production hours for Indonesian sample firms; Lee, Anas, and Oh, 1999) or a higher unit cost for power, due to the necessity of purchasing and running a private generator. Because of the substantial nature of (lost) scale economies in electricity production, the additional cost can be substantial. Lee and his colleagues note that, faced with deficient infrastructure, firms essentially have four options: 1) they can move to another urban place; 2) they can attempt to substitute the infrastructure input by another factor input (i.e., labour or another capital good); 3) they can implement their own private provision; or 4) reduce or stop output. Option 1 is generally of little avail (other cities in nation X will not necessarily be much better); option 2 is largely constrained by technology; option 4 is more difficult to measure.

Lee and his colleagues observe that option 3 was by far the dominant response in cases of severe infrastructure deficiency. Thus, in Nigeria, some 92% of the firms sampled had their own generators and about 44% had dug their own boreholes (for water); the figures for Indonesia were, respectively, 65% and 60% (for artesian wells). Lee et al. also looked at the extra costs for purchasing radio equipment, cell phones, etc., as a substitute for deficient telecommunications infrastructure, and the cost of vehicles for workers where public transit systems were deficient. Many of these types of infrastructure involve high fixed costs, which explains why Lee and his colleagues find that the combined cost of privately provided services is proportionally much higher for smaller firms than it is for larger ones: in Nigeria, 30.5% for smaller firms, 13.3% for large firms: Lee, Anas, and Oh (1999: Table 3.1). If one assumes that small enterprises are more labour-intensive, this situation implies that fewer jobs are being generated.

In sum, the infrastructure deficiencies observed by Lee and his colleagues clearly have a dampening effect on agglomeration economies and contribute to explain the lower productivity of many developing cities. The focus of Lee and his colleagues is on what we have called "hard" infrastructure, where private provision is an alternative response, (via privatized public utility or self-provision). The privatization alternative probably explains why "hard" infrastructure has been the focus of many studies and policy initiatives (not least by the World Bank). At least there is an alternative. If the public sector cannot do the job properly, then why not turn it over to the private (or community) sector? Mainly because localized public services do not have a private counterpart. "Pure" localized public services are often intangible, their impacts on production costs being often indirect and difficult to quantify.

Pure Localized Public Goods

Many localized services are "pure" public goods that cannot be privately provided. The private sector can build roads, streets, lampposts, parks, police stations, fire stations, traffic lights, etc. Government can subcontract services such as road maintenance, street cleaning, refuse collection, and even policing and fire fighting. However, in all cases (with the possible exception of refuse collection), the public sector must in the end pay the subcontractor, establish the regulations that govern the service, and monitor outcomes. By the same token, planning and regulation of land must be assured by the public sector[8]. This holds equally for the regulations and pricing systems (taxes, permits, etc.) that govern both public and private transportation. Again, the private sector may well build (and sometimes also maintain) roads and highways, but the state must decide where they go and establish the institutional framework that oversees them. The planning and management of public spaces (squares, green spaces, etc.) must fall to the public sector. Other examples include the by-laws, regulations, and fiscal incentives that govern the architectural aesthetics of the city (frontage and building height, rights-of-way, design, heritage conservation, etc.). In all cases, these are services for which the consumer cannot be directly charged. The private sector has little incentive to provide them.

The dependence of agglomeration economies on pure public goods is easy to illustrate. The movement of people and goods within cities requires roads, streets, sidewalks, public lighting, public order and traffic control. Only the public sector can provide these services, although limited cases of private provision may exist, for example, restricted private developments (i.e., gated communities) with their own police, or industrial estates (industrial parks) with their own infrastructure.

However, such private provision is geographically limited, restricted to the area enclosed by the residential development or industrial park. Beyond their borders, the user is again at the mercy of the public sector. Unlike most types of "hard" infrastructure (water, power, telecommunications), which firms may choose to privately provide for themselves, albeit at higher costs, as we have seen, the option of private supply does not exist for pure localized public services. A firm can do little about poor road conditions, traffic congestion or crime beyond its walls. Urban places where interaction is costly due to deficient urban planning, crime or traffic congestion will, in sum, generate lower agglomeration economies.

Localized public services and the institutions that provide them are the focus of this study. We follow Lee's methodology to measure the private costs of deficiencies in local public services. However, in the cases of pure public goods, we cannot measure the additional costs that self-provision imposes on firms (for example, lost scale economies in power provision).

As noted earlier, pure localized public services are more difficult to quantify than "hard" localized public services. They are generally intangible or invisible; their impact on production costs is often indirect, through lost time and opportunities.

Illustrating the Costs of Inferior Pure Localized Public Services

Table 1.2 provides examples of impacts of inferior localized public services on production costs for firms. Table 1.2 also gives examples of "coping strategies," which indirectly imply additional costs. The costs posited include all economic costs, including opportunity costs, which ultimately translate into "real" costs for the firm in terms of lower productivity and lost markets. However, the concept of "economic cost" is not easily grasped by entrepreneurs and managers in the field. Looking at the cost headings, "Transport of Goods," we see not only the direct costs of transporting a unit of product X between two points, but also the indirect costs to the firm of delays in the delivery of inputs and outputs, the cost of damaged goods (inputs and outputs), additional vehicle repair and replacement costs due to poor street conditions and congestion, plus the costs attributable to the variability (unreliability) of deliveries.

By the same token, the range of costs under the heading of "Public Safety" includes the psychological costs of personal insecurity to workers, management, and their families. The cost of high crime rates is doubled: first, costs are borne by those directly affected; second, there are indirect costs in terms of lost work opportunities. In a city where people fear to travel at night (especially women), evening and night shifts will be more difficult to implement, which in turn raises unit production costs, in cases where fixed capital costs are significant. Crime and fear of crime can affect the use of the city at various levels: it can affect the overall potential for interaction and exchange. This is an increasing concern not only in developing cities but also in industrialized ones (Gates and Rohe, 1987; Thomas and Bromley, 2000).

The costs associated with dealing with an inefficient local public administration, including time lost, frustration, paper work, corruption and arbitrary decision-making, are subsumed under the heading "Public Administration." The combined

Table 1.2: Localized Public Services: Possible Impacts on Production Costs

Service	Examples of costs due to poor services (and how firms cope)
Transport of Goods Maintenance and repair of local road and street network Traffic control and safety	*Costs* Delays: impact on production runs and customer service. Increased vehicle repairs and fuel costs due to poor road conditions. Higher insurance premiums on vehicles. Goods damaged or spoiled due to delays. Higher personnel costs (drivers, mechanics). *Coping strategies* Deliveries are made at night or early morning to avoid congestion. Purchase sturdier vehicles.
Movement of Persons Management and security of public transit systems Maintenance and repair of local road and street network Traffic control and safety Public parking	*Costs* Employee lateness: work time lost. Employee stress and fatigue: effects on productivity. For business travel: time lost, reduced possibilities for management and customer meetings, impact on managerial efficiency. Information lost. *Coping strategies* Establishments provide transportation for their employees. Establishments adjust employee work shifts (hours). Executives avoid planning more than one (out-of-office) business meeting per day.
Public Safety Local police enforcement Public lighting and surveillance Public firefighting services	*Costs* Theft/damage of goods and equipment, injuries to personnel or customers, higher insurance premiums (including fire), cost of private security services and protection devices, psychological costs (stress / insecurity), impacts on labour productivity, production time (and /or) markets lost because of stolen or damaged goods, difficulty in hiring and keeping labour (especially female) due to safety considerations, difficult (or impossible) to have work shifts during non-daylight hours. *Coping strategies* Establishments hire private protection services and purchase protection devices. Establishments contribute to the local police and /or contract out for private fire protection services.
Public Administration, Basic Services and Local Bylaws Administration of local zoning codes and bylaws Water and sanitation services Solid waste collection and disposal Local permits and inspection (fire, construction, sanitation, etc.)	*Costs* For zoning, bylaws and permits: insecurity of tenure, time lost on negotiations and dealings with public officials, arbitrary decision process, negative impacts on planning and investment. Time (and production) lost waiting for permits and public service connections. For water: variability in pressure, unreliability, need to provide own water. Need to provide own waste disposal services. Health risks to employees. *Coping strategies* Establishments hire persons to deal with local authorities. Establishments provide own services (i.e., water, sanitation). Establishments contribute to local political parties or make other contributions to public officials.

efficiency of all localized public services (no matter which public agency provides them) will determine the agglomeration economies available to firms in a given urban place. Since agglomeration economies are externalities (their gains originate outside the firm), the ability of local firms to create income and employment does not depend on their behaviour alone but also on a broad range of external factors woven into the urban environment. Pure localized public services are but one of these factors. In the following chapters we attempt to better measure their contribution.

CONCLUSION

We reviewed the relationship between agglomeration and economic growth, and concluded that the link was not automatic. Cities (agglomerations, urban places) will not, by their mere presence or size, trigger economic growth unless other conditions are also present. The fact that some urban places do not generate the full "allocational" gains (static agglomeration economies) that one might expect can be explained by the importance of national policies, institutions, culture, and values in the overall productivity level of a given urban agglomeration or city at a given moment in time. It is clear that local institutions and inferior localized public services, necessarily tied to place, have an impact on the productivity of urban firms.

Our evaluation of the importance of "pure" localized public services stems from their links with agglomeration economies. The ability to interact more efficiently (to trade, commute and communicate) lies at the heart of the potential benefits to be gained from agglomeration. If the city does not provide a "productive" setting where interaction and transactions are facilitated (due, say, to high crime, poor traffic management or an insecure regulatory environment) then the potential gains from agglomeration will be lower. The services we examine in the following chapters (see Table 1.2) all affect the ability of economic agents to "productively" interact in the city. If, for example, people cannot move freely within the city to meet, exchange ideas, and learn from each other, then all the potential productivity gains that knowledge spillovers (associated with agglomeration economies) should generate will not materialize.

We do not wish to suggest that localized public services are more important than other policy areas, such as health, education, sound fiscal and monetary policies, etc. They are part of the complex mix of public policies and institutions that determine national economic performance. However, their relative importance grows as a nation becomes more urbanized. This may, in part, explain why some nations find it difficult to ensure further growth once a given level of urbanization has been attained. Localized public services have their own problems because they cannot easily be corrected by centralized public action or national legislation. Their efficacy ultimately rests on the shoulders of hundreds (thousands) of localized public servants and many more private citizens. This brings to mind Howe's (1915) reference to "co-operation in a million unseen ways" needed to make the modern city work. The nature of localized public services, as "pure" public goods, means that their delivery is intimately linked to the overall functioning of the state, and also, to what we may term the revealing local "civic culture."

Notes

[1]   Taken from Kuznets (1968): 6.

[2]   The reader is also referred to modern textbooks such as Mills and Hamilton (1994) and O'Sullivan (2000) in English, or Polèse (1994, 1998a, 1998b) in French, Spanish and Portuguese. For a more in-depth analysis, especially from an economic theoretical perspective, see Fujita and Thisse (2002).

[3]   For different firms in different industrial sectors, the trade-off between the gains and the costs of agglomeration (primarily congestion, land and labor costs) will partly determine the size of the urban area in which they locate. This, in turn, helps to explain why industries do not concentrate in one single (huge) agglomeration (Henderson, 1997).

[4]   Econometric studies, which model the relationship between knowledge spillovers, innovation and cities, are generally based on U.S. data and sometimes, but more rarely, on European or Japanese sources. A discussion of the models and indicators used falls beyond the purview of this chapter.

[5]   Criteria may vary among nations.

[6]   Heer (1962: 82) notes that elements of Venetian constitutional practice were absorbed into the constitutions of many U.S. states where, in altered form, they have survived.

[7]   Their point is almost a negative one: they argue that the relatively inefficient functioning of certain Indian industrial sectors in large cities, i.e., negative agglomeration economies, can partly be explained by the underdeveloped nature of India's transport infrastructure. Underdeveloped links to smaller and medium-sized cities push industries to "artificially" concentrate in the largest cities, despite congestion costs and other agglomeration diseconomies. Given the limited transport links, only the largest cities offer adequate market access under current conditions. However, one might argue that there is a circular relation between scale (city size), intercity trade and traffic volume, and unit transport costs.

[8]   Land use planning and building codes are, for example, essential in reducing the potential damage of "natural" disasters, such as earthquakes, hurricanes, volcanoes, floods, etc. It is no coincidence that it is often the poorest "unregulated" areas that suffer most. In many cases, much of the damage could have been avoided.

CHAPTER 2

Research Strategy and Methodology

The work by Lee and his associates on the private impact of public infrastructure deficiencies (see references cited in Chapter 1) served as our chief point of departure. Based on the questionnaires used by Lee et al. in Thailand, Indonesia and Nigeria, on other questionnaires used in industry surveys, both in the North and in developing countries, and drawing on the literature review (Chapter 1), the research team prepared a questionnaire and survey strategy. The basic survey tool was the same in each of the five cities studied but the strategies were adapted to local conditions.

1. THE CHOICE OF CITIES AND INTER-CITY COORDINATION

Five cities were included in the study, based on the presence of competent local research centers, knowledgeable in the area of urban economics and field research: Belo Horizonte, Brazil; Montreal, Canada; Puebla, Mexico; San José, Costa Rica; San Salvador, El Salvador. The three Hispanic cities are of comparable size: urban agglomerations of approximately 1.5 million inhabitants. Belo Horizonte and Montreal are considerably larger with, respectively, metropolitan populations of about 4.5 million and 3.4 million. In all cases, the urban area refers to the greater metropolitan area, although the precise criteria used to define metropolitan areas may vary between nations.

Given our research objectives, the strategy was to use Montreal, our only Northern case, as the reference point to which the results for the four developing cities would be compared. Montreal was chosen mainly because, like most Canadian cities, it is reputed to be generally well-managed, to have good public services and infrastructure, and an honest and competent local civil service.

The various stages of the research (questionnaire, sampling procedures, discussion group template, analysis of results, etc.) were elaborated collectively with input from all researchers. The five city teams and research coordinators met six times during the course of the project, with the first meeting held in San José, in February 2001, and the last meeting in Washington, D.C., in December 2002. General coordination and logistics were the responsibility of the Montreal team. By general agreement, the working language of all meetings was Spanish, as well the primary language of written coordination (i.e., the minutes of meetings). However, written communication could also be in English or Portuguese, given that all senior researchers had at least a passive (reading) knowledge of all three languages.

2. SAMPLE SELECTION: ESTABLISHMENT CHARACTERISTICS

To maximize comparability, the survey sought, as far as possible, to cover the same industries in each city. We thus needed to identify industries that were represented in sufficient numbers in all five cities. Given the industrial structure of the five cities, two sectors were identified: food processing and apparel (clothing). Initially, the pharmaceutical industry, present in the five cities, was also considered, but eventually rejected, both because of the small number of firms in some cities and its reputation for secrecy. To further ensure comparability, we decided to examine establishments of comparable size. However, this necessarily implies that there is existing data on the size, characteristics and distribution of business establishments within each urban area. Proper sampling requires some knowledge of the population (universe) at large. Such data is difficult to obtain, if at all, even for most industrialized cities. Different sources were used in different cities to obtain basic data on the numbers and characteristics of establishments: Chambers of Commerce, professional associations, municipal tax roles, statistical agencies, telephone directories, etc. Data was particularly hard to come by in San Salvador and Belo Horizonte[1]. On the basis of the available data, it was decided that the surveys should concentrate on establishments with 40 to 300 employees. However, because of the discrepancy between initial information (industry lists) and the actual data obtained, some establishments surveyed fell outside this range[2]. In addition, because of response problems (most notably in Belo Horizonte), a point to which we shall return, researchers were sometimes forced to survey establishments falling outside this range[3].

In all cases, the unit of observation is the establishment, that is, an identifiable place of business (a plant or workshop, in most cases) with a separate civic address. This will be different from the "firm," where the establishment is part of a larger multi-establishment enterprise or network. This definition caused no major problem. Thus, all results analyzed in Chapter 4 refer to establishments at given locations. All establishments surveyed, with minor exceptions, were located within the confines of the urban area (agglomeration) as defined by a national statistical agency or similar authority. The only exceptions concerned establishments located at the outer fringes of the urban area, but close enough to warrant inclusion in the sample. In total, some 700 establishments were contacted in the five cities (see Table 2.1), and 165 questionnaires had been completed by the end of the process[4]. We shall return to the issue of low response rates below.

3. SURVEY TOOLS

Two methods were used: a questionnaire and a discussion group template. The full questionnaire and the template may be found, respectively, in Appendices 1 and 2. In the following sections, we describe the content and rationale for each instrument.

Table 2.1: Response Rates by City

City	Establishments contacted [a]	Questionnaires sent out and / or visits scheduled [b]	Questionnaires received / filled out [c]	Response rate 1 [b/a]	Response rate 2 [c/b]
Belo Horizonte	96	96	21	100%	22%
Puebla	99	99	45	100%	45%
San José	114	102	35	89%	34%
San Salvador	74	74	45	100%	61%
Montreal	300	276	19	92%	7%

The Questionnaire

The principal objective of the questionnaire was to quantify the possible impacts on establishments of inferior localized public services, as illustrated in Table 1.2, Chapter 1. To deal with indirect impacts (for example, the impact of traffic congestion on deliveries, and in turn on production), questions were grouped into two classes: 1) factual questions, i.e., "How often did deliveries arrive late;" and 2) evaluation questions, i.e., "What was the impact of late deliveries on production?" As expected, most establishments found it easier to respond to factual questions than evaluation questions. The more indirect the impact, the more difficult it was for establishments to evaluate its effect and cost.

To test the field and methodology, a series of pilot surveys, with a longer version of the questionnaire, were carried out in the five cities during the months of October and November 2001. Following the results of the pilots and a meeting of the research team, the questionnaire was reduced to seventeen pages.

The questionnaire is divided into six parts. The first part deals with basic identification and financial questions. The next four sections deal with the services outlined in Table 1.2 (Chapter 1): movement of goods, movement of persons, public safety, local public administration, and local regulatory framework. A sixth section was added to deal with a subset of the movement of persons, that is, the movement of executives, managers, etc., within the city, for purposes of business meetings and face-to-face contacts. As noted in Chapter 1, one of the primary attributes of agglomeration economies, i.e., the gains from agglomeration, is the facilitation of interaction and interpersonal communication. The section dealing with local public administration and local regulatory framework was the most problematic, due to the heterogeneity of public services included in this group and to the difficulty of isolating the factors that impact on the quality of the regulatory framework, such as corruption, poor staffing, arbitrary power, lack of clear rules, etc.

Discussion Groups

To strengthen the results of the research and to control the responses of the questionnaire, focus groups were organized in three cities to validate the questionnaire results.

With the help of an expert[5], specializing in focus group and Delphi techniques, various iterations of the template were reviewed and exchanged between the five city teams before arriving at a final product. These interactions were necessary to ensure cross-cultural coherence. Because many respondents had difficulty assessing the cost implications of inferior public services, it was decided that this question would be emphasized during the focus groups. Section 5 of the questionnaire was subdivided into two parts: a) basic urban services and b) the regulatory framework as such. The strategy selected for the discussion groups focused on using the template to guide participants, one service at a time, to a better understanding of the concept of underlying cost, and then to ask them to suggest a cost estimate. At the end of each session, the cost estimates were collectively revisited.

The approach used in the discussion groups was a combination of focus groups and Delphi, within a very tight schedule. During the research, it was clear that business persons are reluctant to participate in an exercise of this nature either because of a tradition of mistrust and lack of communication, or because they saw little personal (or business) interest in participating. To take advantage of the presence of key businesspeople in these meetings, it was essential to keep the discussion group meetings short and focused. The discussion groups in each city were scheduled as breakfast meetings in a well-known hotel and were planned to run for no more than two hours. Personal invitations were sent out to selected business persons, about a dozen in each case, chosen among those who were most cooperative during the first phase. Here again, response rates varied considerably between cities.

The discussion group technique was used in the three Hispanic cities (Puebla, San José and San Salvador), with one meeting per industry, two per city. In each case, the discussions were chaired by the same moderator[6], who had previously undergone training in Montreal. A discussion guide was prepared for the chair's use, in order to further ensure homogeneity. In addition, each prospective participant was sent a paper copy of the (PowerPoint) template and an instruction sheet in preparation for the meeting. Not withstanding the discipline imposed by the template and the chair, the discussion group technique allowed sufficient flexibility for the expression of different opinions.

On the whole, we found this to be a very useful (and cost effective) tool, partly because it allowed us to better comprehend the cultural and subjective aspects of some questions, but also because it allowed us to interpret the survey results in a more realistic light, given local conditions. One of the major conclusions drawn from this exercise is that discussion groups should precede a full-scale survey to help focus and sharpen the relevant questions for the group.

4. SURVEY STRATEGIES: ADMINISTERING THE QUESTIONNAIRE

As earlier indicated, different survey strategies were used in different cities, with varying degrees of success (Table 2.1). Initially, a common strategy, which all city research teams were to use, was elaborated (Table 2.2). However, the various teams adjusted the initial plan in response to local conditions and realities, as will become clearer in the following paragraphs.

In the cases of San José and Puebla, trained survey-takers (generally students with some previous survey experience) went to the establishments to fill out the questionnaires. Each visit was preceded by: a) a first visit, in which a formal letter was delivered, describing the purpose of the survey; and b) a follow-up telephone call to gauge the potential respondent's interest, set a meeting time in the case of a positive response, and gather basic data[7]. In many cases, repeated telephone calls, often by a senior researcher, were required to gain agreement. However, in all cases prior consent was sought. As Table 2.1 indicates, this was the most successful strategy, but also the most labour-intensive and time-consuming. By the same token, the information gathered in Puebla and San José showed itself to be very robust, precisely because the questionnaires were generally filled out by trained survey-takers.

In San Salvador, as in Belo Horizonte, the survey was administered using intermediaries, an indication, perhaps, of different research climates and institutional cultures. In San Salvador, the questionnaires for the clothing industry were distributed via the Ministry of Economy, which sent them out and collected them. Questionnaires for the food-processing industry were contracted out to students, who visited the establishments, following initial contacts by the Department of Economics of the Universidad José Simeon Cañas (UCA). As Table 2.1 indicates, establishments in San Salvador were often reluctant to respond. Also, where firms did participate, they were generally highly discreet in their responses, especially for questions dealing with financial matters. Belo Horizonte proved to be the most difficult case. Despite the best efforts of the local research team, it was impossible to organize a survey for the food-processing industry. In Belo Horizonte, it seems, any survey requires the prior approval (and subsequent monitoring) of the local industry association. Direct surveys without some sort of "official" intermediary are, it would appear, simply not part of the culture. The survey for the clothing industry was thus administered via the clothing industry union of Minas Gerais (SINDEST).

For Montreal, the initial strategy was similar to the one employed in Puebla and San José: a letter, followed by a telephone call and a visit. However, the response to the first step was so low that alternative strategies were put into place to motivate establishments to respond. The problem in Montreal was clearly one of lack of motivation (and not lack of trust as in other cities). Among the strategies used were: a second letter, via e-mail, with the endorsement of the Montreal Board of Trade, plus a posting on its Web site; repeated follow-up telephone calls; a Web site where establishments could directly fill out the questionnaire; numerous mailings of the questionnaire (both paper and e-mail). Despite all this, the total number of questionnaires received remained disappointingly low. On the other hand, the questionnaires received in Montreal were generally very complete and with few missing items.

Given the small size of the sample, the exercise does not have full statistical representativeness. The small number of cases has also reduced the econometric analysis. A correlation matrix, on the basis of 165 observations (total of all cities), is depicted in Table 2.3. While few coefficients are truly significant, most signs go in the expected direction. When correlated with "output per employee," the coefficient for the Montreal dummy is positive (+0.51), significant, and, as would be expected, by far the highest coefficient. The other variables that significantly correlate with output per employee are "neighbourhood security" (+0.33), "composite impact of

Table 2.2: Proposed Stages for the Survey (with Variants by City)

	Stage	Variations by City
1	Identification of establishments.	Local team defines the sample.
2	If possible, identify key contact in each establishment.	According to available information.
3	Send invitation letter to the establishment.	• By mail in Montreal and email when possible. • In the other cities: according to local conditions. It may be delivered in person. • Delivery of the letter will be preceded by a telephone call, where useful (and possible).
4	Establish contact with establishment to know if they are willing to participate in the survey, and (if positive answer): • Identify the key person; • Determine the conditions for sending the questionnaire; • If necessary, give additional explanations on the way to filling out the questionnaire; • Set up an appointment for an interview as well as to pick up the completed questionnaires.	• In Montreal: by telephone (+ sometimes email) for the contact. Delivery of questionnaires by mail. • In the other cities: according to the quality of telecommunications and local traditions. • We propose that two (2) questionnaires be sent to each establishment, one with loose leafs for Section 6. Different people will often fill out Section 6. Another possibility: to send 6 questionnaires.
5	Deliver questionnaires and confirm appointment (for approximately one week later) to pick up completed questionnaires.	Follows from the previous stage, with same comments.
6	• Pick up completed questionnaires. • Set up an interview with key contact for the following week.	Done in person, everywhere.
7	First verification of the questionnaire. Recopy information of the separate parts onto a single questionnaire. If necessary, identify inconsistencies or missing information.	Same procedure everywhere. It is possible (in Stage 6) that certain people may take more time causing delays. The missing information will have to be completed during an interview or, alternately, see Stage 8.
8	Confirm appointment for interview 24 hours before the agreed date. If problem, reschedule the appointment and restart procedure.	• In Montreal, by phone or email. • In other cities: according to quality of telecommunications.
9	Interview with the key contact or person referred by contact. The interview may last 30-45 minutes.	
10	If necessary, make new contact with the key person in establishment to correct inconsistencies and missing information.	Here, procedure is not standard. It will depend on the quality of telecommunications as well as the extent of errors and inconsistencies
11	Last verification, codification of the answers.	
12	Enter corresponding data for each establishment in computer file. This file contains a matrix that will be the same for all cities.	SPSS may be used but information must be stored in an Excel file for final treatment of the data.

missed business meetings[8]" (-0.34), and the Belo Horizonte dummy (-0.24), where the latter is, in part, a reflection of the smaller size, on average, of establishments in Belo Horizonte (see Chapter 4, Figure 4.1.2).

In the following two chapters, we present, in turn, the results of the discussion groups in the three Hispanic cities and the survey administered in five cities. Given, in each case, the small sample sizes, the contribution of our analysis is, admittedly, primarily descriptive. However, as we shall see, the mixture of descriptive and qualitative analyses nonetheless reveals many useful insights.

Notes

[1] More information on sampling problems can be found in the relevant city chapters.

[2] Thus, for example, the initial list (obtained, say, from the local Chamber of Commerce) might indicate an establishment's size as 50 (employees), while the survey revealed that the current level of employment is in fact at 30.

[3] Median establishment size was considerably smaller in Belo Horizonte than in other cities: see Chapter 4.

[4] For the distribution of respondents among cities, see Figure 4.1.1 in Chapter 4.

[5] Vincent Dumas.

[6] Judith Chaffee, Professor and ex-chair, Department of Economics, Universidad Autónoma de Puebla.

[7] The precise procedure may vary, depending on technology and on the characteristics of the establishment. Thus, in some cases, the first step (letter) was done by e-mail or fax. In some cases, telephone calls (or e-mail contacts) preceded the delivery of the formal letter. In other cases, the first visit allowed the student to immediately set a meeting.

[8] See Chapter 4 (Figure 4.3.9) for an explanation of this variable.

Table 2.3a: Correlation Matrix for all Five Cities

	Belo Horizonte	Montreal	Puebla	San José	San Salvador	clothing	center	opening year	owner reside	out region	out country	nb employee	% female	sale employee
Belo Horizonte	1													
Montreal	-0.14	1												
Puebla	-0.23	-0.22	1											
San José	-0.20	-0.19	-0.32	1										
San Salvador	-0.23	-0.22	-0.38	-0.32	1									
clothing	0.31	-0.06	-0.20	-0.19	0.19	1								
center	a	-0.04	0.08	-0.04	-0.01	0.01	1							
opening year	0.19	-0.14	0.06	-0.36	0.23	0.46	-0.06	1						
owner reside	0.06	-0.01	-0.01	-0.12	0.07	0.18	0.04	0.13	1					
out region	-0.30	0.15	-0.09	-0.16	0.40	0.20	-0.03	0.03	0.05	1				
out country	-0.29	0.03	-0.18	-0.10	0.53	0.34	-0.06	0.16	-0.04	0.74	1			
nb employee	-0.17	-0.13	-0.05	-0.08	0.35	-0.02	-0.07	-0.07	-0.20	0.26	0.22	1		
% female	.(a)	0.12	0.06	-0.22	0.08	0.55	-0.12	0.21	0.11	0.09	0.12	0.06	1	
sale employee	-0.14	0.53	-0.10	-0.09	-0.10	-0.08	0.07	-0.23	0.01	0.15	-0.02	-0.09	-0.03	1
prod employee	-0.24	0.51	-0.02	-0.10	-0.06	-0.18	-0.06	-0.16	-0.05	0.08	0.04	-0.05	-0.10	0.74
late deliveries	-0.21	-0.06	0.04	0.13	0.06	-0.08	0.01	-0.02	-0.20	0.11	0.16	0.14	-0.13	0.05
road impact	-0.13	-0.19	0.04	0.13	0.07	-0.11	0.25	-0.07	0.09	-0.15	0.00	-0.02	-0.05	-0.11
congestion impact	-0.16	-0.12	-0.17	0.39	0.01	-0.15	0.19	-0.23	0.11	-0.06	0.01	0.02	-0.13	-0.09
empl late	-0.30	-0.16	0.12	0.12	0.12	0.01	0.02	-0.02	-0.02	0.12	0.17	0.05	0.03	-0.13
security pers	0.07	-0.18	0.03	0.04	0.02	0.14	0.12	-0.04	-0.13	-0.02	-0.14	-0.05	0.20	-0.11
safe neigbourhood	-0.38	0.21	0.14	0.10	-0.12	-0.25	-0.08	-0.03	0.05	0.25	0.23	-0.15	-0.15	0.20
crime operation	0.18	-0.02	-0.01	-0.16	0.05	0.10	0.12	0.01	0.14	0.00	-0.15	-0.08	0.11	-0.08
retention female	0.29	-0.01	0.01	-0.15	-0.10	0.20	0.16	0.05	0.05	-0.13	-0.14	-0.06	0.09	0.01
impact transport	-0.12	-0.06	-0.19	0.21	0.15	-0.11	0.18	-0.10	0.03	-0.05	-0.02	0.23	-0.39	-0.12
imp. empl. transp.	-0.02	-0.04	-0.06	-0.02	0.13	0.19	0.00	0.10	0.17	0.11	0.15	0.09	0.12	-0.14
impact security	0.34	-0.11	-0.24	-0.08	0.25	0.12	0.19	0.00	-0.01	-0.25	-0.16	-0.05	-0.06	-0.07
impact regulation	0.02	-0.17	-0.03	-0.00	0.19	-0.02	0.06	0.07	0.07	0.09	0.11	-0.03	0.06	-0.08
index security	0.30	-0.15	0.13	-0.23	-0.02	0.17	0.18	0.07	0.06	-0.13	-0.20	0.01	0.20	-0.12
index reunions	0.31	-0.21	-0.04	-0.06	0.21	0.20	0.21	0.27	0.05	-0.12	-0.05	-0.09	-0.08	-0.19
index assault	0.27	-0.21	-0.04	-0.19	0.17	0.18	-0.07	0.19	-0.07	-0.12	-0.15	0.16	0.15	-0.15
index theft	-0.02	0.13	0.02	0.12	-0.21	-0.08	0.04	-0.16	-0.14	-0.07	-0.09	0.07	-0.04	0.08

Correlation is significant at the 0.01 level   Correlation is significant at the 0.05 level
a. Cannot be computed (at least one variable is constant)

Table 2.3a (Continued)

prod employee	late deliveries	road impact	congestion impact	empl late	security pers	safe neigh-bourhood	crime operation	retention female	impact transport	impact empl transport	impact security	impact regulation	index security	index reunions	index assault	index theft
1																
0.13	1															
-0.12	0.23	1														
-0.04	0.13	0.48	1													
0.03	0.09	0.14	0.16	1												
-0.17	0.00	-0.11	-0.09	0.13	1											
0.33	0.10	0.04	-0.08	0.07	0.06	1										
-0.12	-0.15	-0.12	0.06	0.01	-0.01	-0.20	1									
-0.11	-0.13	-0.15	-0.02	-0.06	-0.02	-0.25	0.34	1								
-0.07	0.13	0.20	0.42	0.13	-0.09	-0.05	0.07	-0.15	1							
-0.10	-0.07	0.25	0.24	0.41	0.11	-0.07	-0.02	-0.09	0.34	1						
-0.08	-0.07	0.06	-0.00	-0.06	0.02	-0.23	0.27	0.05	0.09	0.13	1					
-0.11	0.07	0.17	0.16	0.05	0.11	-0.10	0.03	-0.13	0.24	0.21	0.02	1				
-0.16	-0.08	0.01	0.01	-0.04	-0.03	-0.36	0.70	0.62	-0.01	-0.05	0.32	0.10	1			
-0.34	0.12	0.19	0.07	0.18	-0.08	-0.20	0.15	0.20	0.21	0.34	0.21	0.13	0.20	1		
-0.18	0.06	-0.03	0.01	-0.09	0.01	-0.42	0.15	0.03	-0.05	-0.02	0.15	0.05	0.19	0.14	1	
0.07	0.29	0.15	0.08	0.05	-0.16	-0.20	0.08	0.19	0.04	-0.04	0.12	-0.04	0.31	-0.01	0.27	1

Table 2.3b: Definition of Variables Used in Correlation Matrix

Name	Definition
[1] Belo Horizonte	dummy variable: Belo Horizonte (0/1)
[2] Montreal	dummy variable: Montreal (0/1)
[3] Puebla	dummy variable: Puebla (0/1)
[4] San José	dummy variable: San José (0/1)
[5] San Salvador	dummy variable: San Salvador (0/1)
[6] clothing	dummy variable: establishments in clothing industry (0/1)
[7] centre	dummy variable: establishments located in centre of the city (0/1)
[8] opening year	continuous variable: begining of operation (year)
[9] owner reside	dummy variable: owner stays in the same metropolitan area as establishment (0/1)
[10] out region	continuous variable: % of sales outside metro area
[11] out country	continuous variable: % of sales outside country
[12] nb employee	continuous variable: number of employees
[13] % female	continuous variable: % of female workers
[14] sale employee	continuous variable: sales/worker
[15] prod employee	continuous variable: production/worker
[16] late deliveries	dummy variable: delivery delays at least once a week (0/1)
[17] road impact	dummy variable: impact of poor road conditions on transport cost: major impact (0/1)
[18] congestion impact	dummy variable: impact of congestion on transport cost: major impact (0/1)
[19] empl late	dummy variable: workers arriving late at least once a week (0/1)
[20] security pers	continuous variable: security related employees/total employees (0/1)
[21] safe neighbourhood	dummy variable: safe neighbourhood (0/1)
[22] crime operation	dummy variable: significant impact of crime and violence on ability to operate at full capacity (0/1)
[23] retention female	dummy variable: significant impact of crime and violence on hiring and retention of female personnel (0/1)
[24] impact transport	continuous variable: overall impact of transport problems on total production cost
[25] impact empl transport	continuous variable: overall impact of employee transport problems on total production cost
[26] impact security	continuous variable: overall impact of security problems on total production cost
[27] impact regulation	continuous variable: overall impact of local regulatory framework on total production cost
[28] index security	continuous variable: composite index of security related problems
[29] index reunions	continuous variable: composite index of missed meetings
[30] index assaults	continuous variable: composite index on assaults with a weapon
[31] index theft	continuous variable: composite index of total thefts

The Impact of Inferior Localized Public Services. Qualitative Analysis: Discussion Group Results

This chapter presents the results obtained in the discussion groups organized in the three Spanish-speaking cities[1]. It also serves as an introduction to the more quantitative chapter to follow, giving a better sense of what lies behind the data.

Introductory Methodological Considerations

The discussion groups were based on a mixed formula, using both focus group and open-ended techniques. The same template (Appendix 2) was used in each case, with the same person leading the discussions. The results reflect the estimates provided by the participants during the discussions and our impressions during the meetings.

Essentially, the business persons participating in the meetings were asked to evaluate the impact of deficient public services on their establishment's costs. To facilitate the process, participants were asked to estimate costs in terms of percentages (of total costs). In each case, a pre-set discussion plan was used to guide the iterative process (see Appendix 2). The concept of "cost" was a bit difficult to understand, especially when it included foregone revenues, opportunities lost (fairly abstract notions), psychological costs, as well as direct financial costs. The difficulty the participants had in understanding the exact concept of overall cost may have led to inaccuracies in the obtained results. The estimates depicted in Tables 3.2 through 3.7 may contain a large element of judgment on the part of the participants and should be interpreted with care.

After putting all the elements together, we believe that the participants' cost estimates underestimate the cost impact of deficient public services. On the one hand, there are great variations in individual assessments, and in no case was a consensus achieved for the industry as a whole. San Salvador participants were not able to suggest any estimates at all (with one exception), restricting their input to qualitative considerations. This is also an indication of a low level of trust in San Salvador, despite the fact that participants were promised anonymity.

No discussion group took place in Montreal. Montreal business people may have been overloaded with similar surveys, and the questions asked may not have been relevant to the Montreal context (with the possible exception of merchandise transport questions). Montreal firms were not interested in the discussion group as the costs we wished to measure were not an issue for them.

Table 3.1: Distribution of Discussion Group Participants by City and Industrial Sector

City	Food Processing	Apparel	Total
Puebla	9	3	12
San José	4	4	8
San Salvador	3	1	4
Total	16	8	24

Twenty-four business persons participated in the various discussion groups held in the three cities (Table 3.1). The low turnout in San Salvador reflects the higher level of mistrust in that city. The food processing sector, which provided the majority of participants, can in turn be divided into two sub-sectors: those producing perishable goods (milk products, baked goods, processed meat products), and those producing canned, bottled or packaged goods. Naturally, the former group is much more sensitive to merchandise transport costs than the latter. This heterogeneity explains, in part, the difficulty of arriving at "representative" figures for the whole industry. Almost all the firms present were domestically owned (either locally controlled or the principal establishment of a national enterprise); only one was under foreign control. This may explain their greater willingness to participate in the discussion groups and, correspondingly, their level of concern with local issues. By the same token, the majority of participants (12) came from smaller establishments, with fewer than 100 employees. Three others represented establishments with 100 to 299 employees, and 7 with 300 or more employees (two remained unidentified).

Because of the small number of participants, we will not distinguish between cities or industrial sectors, but rather concentrate on general observations.

Preliminary Conclusions

In our literature review, we made reference to what we may refer to as Lee's four options model (Lee, Anas and Oh, 1999). Briefly stated, in the face of inferior service, firms have four options: 1) they can move to another location; 2) they can attempt to substitute the service with another factor input; 3) they can choose private and/or self-provision; or 4) choose output reduction or cessation. Lee and his associates, who specifically looked at "hard" local public services, concluded that options 1 and 2 were rarely feasible, and that the burden of implementing option 3 was generally greater for smaller firms, with an obvious negative impact on startup businesses. In this respect, it is useful to mention three points that repeatedly came out of the discussion groups:

1. The costs resulting from inferior (or absent) localized public services affect smaller firms proportionally more than larger firms. When added together, the direct and indirect costs (time lost, cost of corruption, administrative hassle, insecurity, etc.) create such a burden that, in many cases, going into business is not a viable option. In sum, the observations of the participants largely

reinforce Lee's conclusions regarding the impact of inferior public services on business startup.

2. Moving to another location was generally not considered an option. Only one case of a business exercising this option was mentioned by a participant. But, even in this case, the establishment in question moved within the same neighbourhood because it did not wish to lose its workforce (see the section on transport of persons).

3. Factor substitution was generally not an option either, given technological constraints. Private (self-) provision, which generally implies higher costs, was naturally only possible for services with existing private-based substitutes, i.e., waste collection, water, self-provided transportation for employees. Again, such options were often beyond the means of smaller firms.

It is thus not surprising that the general mood in all three cities was one of resignation to the situation. In the majority of cases, the costs suggested in the discussion template (Appendix 2) were considered costs over which the establishment had little control. The general reaction for all classes of services was not so much one of weighing how costs could be lowered or services improved (by lobbying local government, for example) but, rather, of evaluating whether local conditions were sufficient to allow the firm to stay in business. The coping strategies described in the following sections were generally seen as second-best solutions that the establishment had no choice but to adopt if it wished to survive.

1. MERCHANDISE TRANSPORT

In all three cities, costs relating to merchandise transport were considered the most important (although we only have estimates for two cities). In all three, road and traffic conditions were considered substantially substandard. In addition to the costs suggested by the discussion template (late deliveries, time lost, truck repair, etc.), other negative impacts were brought to our attention, most notably the high level of traffic accidents (and personal injuries). This, in turn, had an impact on insurance costs, driver stress, and the number of vehicles out of circulation or in need of repair. Also, the poor design of streets and the absence of clear traffic signs and street names (especially in San José) translated not only into time wasted, but also meant that drivers require additional training. Fanciful parking regulations, often enforced in a more-or-less arbitrary manner also translate into additional costs.

The impact of inferior services on cost ranges from a low of 0.4% (food processing in Puebla) to a high of 15% (apparel in Puebla), with means and medians varying between 2% and 7% of total operating cost (Table 3.2). Cost estimates are very sensitive to establishment characteristics, both with respect to markets and to products. Establishments serving local markets, where trucks must use city streets and often cross central areas, are more affected than those exporting to international or out-of-region markets. The latter have the option of locating at some distance from the centre, often along a highway leading to a port or a national distribution centre. Thus, in the case of Puebla, it is not surprising that the most important industrial zones are located along the Mexico City–Veracruz highway. A similar pattern has evolved in San José, where the chief industrial zones are located along the highway leading to the airport and the port city of Punto Arenas.

Table 3.2: Estimated Impact of Inferior Service on Costs [% of Total Operating Cost]: Merchandise Transport

Values	Puebla		San José	
	Apparel	Food Processing	Apparel	Food Processing
Mean	7.0	3.7	3.0	6.3
Median	5.0	2.0	3.0	5.0
Minimum	1.0	0.4	1.0	5.0
Maximum	15.0	10.0	5.0	10.0

However, this option is not necessarily open to establishments serving local markets, especially when a significant percentage of deliveries are made downtown. Here again, smaller establishments appear to bear the brunt of inferior service, since these establishments are more often located near the centre (often founded there) and smaller establishments are, by definition, more locally oriented. The coping strategies take various forms. Faced with parking problems and constant downtown congestion, some establishments have chosen to make deliveries with smaller vehicles, including motorcycles. Some participants felt that this increased their costs, leading to a duplication of vehicles (where fewer might have sufficed), resulting, in essence, in a loss of scale economies. However, others felt that this was a profitable strategy, allowing them to better adjust their deliveries to changing market demand. However, all participants agreed that poor road conditions translated into additional truck repair costs, plus the need to buy sturdier (and more expensive) vehicles.

The most important cost nonetheless was time lost due to congestion and poor traffic management, both for deliveries and for goods received. In terms of direct costs, extended trips due to slower traffic translate into a higher gasoline cost. The importance of lost-time costs for some establishments may be observed by the willingness of some participants to pay substantially higher wages to drivers with the experience and know-how to deal with existing traffic and road conditions. Some establishments also intentionally maintain a diversified fleet of trucks and vehicles in order to be able to adapt to changing traffic conditions. Among the most common coping strategies is making deliveries (or receiving goods) at off-hours. This, in turn, requires that establishments at the other end of the line be equally open to receiving or delivering merchandise at all hours. However, the feasibility of this option was severely limited by security considerations in all three cities. Making deliveries at night, or in the early morning hours is very costly to implement where public order and safety cannot be ensured, if only in terms of the additional wages (and other benefits) needed to induce drivers to work at night (see also the section below on public safety[2]). Public security considerations make it difficult, if not impossible, for local authorities to implement policies regulating the flow of trucks, i.e., limiting their use to off-hours. In San José, in the hope of reducing congestion, municipal authorities recently proposed restricting the access of heavy trucks to the city during specific hours. The proposal, however, never came into effect, given the strong resistance of the business community.

In San Salvador, local authorities collect a special tax on gasoline (0.05 $ per gallon at the time of writing), which goes into a road fund called Fovial. Although participants considered this a step in the right direction, they also felt the funds collected to be insufficient, indicating as proof the large sums they continue to spend on truck repair and replacement. However, the primary complaint in all three cities did not so much deal with specific cost issues, but rather with the overall absence of rational transportation and land-use planning, an aspect that does not easily lend itself to quantitative analysis. The issue of transportation and land-use planning, in turn, links to broader issues of urban governance, from which considerations of public trust or, inversely, corruption (especially with respect to land development and public contracts), are not totally absent.

2. MOVEMENT OF PERSONS

Overall, costs related to the movement of persons (employees or managers) were considered less important, perhaps because a large part of those costs are borne by the persons themselves. With the exception of (few) cases where the establishment pays transportation for its employees (either by providing it directly or financially compensating employees), costs are indirect and thus difficult to grasp. Participants admitted that they found it difficult to estimate a clear quantitative relation between indirect costs (absenteeism, lateness, etc.) and operating costs, which was not say that these costs were not recognized. In any event, estimates of costs related to inferior personnel transportation services varied from a minimum of zero to a maximum of 5% with means and medians varying between 0.3% and 5% (Table 3.3).

Table 3.3: Estimated Impact of Inferior Service on Costs [% of Total Operating Cost]: Movement of Persons

Values	Puebla		San José	
	Apparel	Food Processing	Apparel	Food Processing
Mean	4.0	1.6	0.4	0.9
Median	5.0	1.0	0.3	1.0
Minimum	2.0	0.1	0.0	0.5
Maximum	5.0	5.0	1.0	1.0

None of the three cities has a publicly financed public transportation service[3], although Puebla does allow credits for vehicle renovation and upgrading for environmental reasons. Routes are privately operated, with a mix of vehicles (combis, colectivos, etc.), as would be expected in cities where demand for public transportation is still high, a corollary of relatively low levels of motorization. In all cities, the sector is regulated with routes, permits, and prices established by the public sector.

In terms of participant satisfaction with the service, the chief difference is between establishments located in or near the centre and those located in more suburban locations. Unlike with merchandise transport, the suburban establishments are most critical of the service.

The primary impact of inferior public transportation services is its effect on employee loyalty and, thus, on employee turnover. This was repeatedly stressed. As such, the indirect costs of high turnover rates, especially where employee training (and/or work experience) directly impacts labour productivity, can be significant. Other participants pointed to lateness and absenteeism as negative impacts, although it is not always possible to distinguish between the effects on employee behaviour of culture and values (for lack of better terms) and of inferior public transportation services. A participant in San Salvador (food processing) stated that his establishment had, on occasion, halted production (or reduced it) because personnel did not show up. Others stated that lateness and absenteeism can threaten the survival of the firm, i.e., its ability to keep market shares, where absent personnel jeopardize not only production runs but also delivery schedules. However, the primary concern remains the impact of inferior public transportation services (especially when added to security issues) on employee turnover.

Coping strategies took various paths. Some mentioned the necessity of adjusting work schedules to the availability of public transportation, the need to plan extra space (for rest or sleep) for workers, and the need to financially compensate employees who work at some distance from the establishment. An establishment in San José (food processing), which previously provided its employees with transportation, now pays them a travel bonus to compensate for the abandoned service. Another establishment in the same city raised employee wages (by approximately $230 annually) to cover commuting costs. An establishment in Puebla (with about 500 employees) provides transportation for its workforce at an approximate annual cost of $10,000. However, very few firms choose to provide transportation for their employees. Also, whether the service was self-provided, or whether the establishment directly paid workers (for commuting costs), such costs were generally felt to be a minor element in the establishment's cost structure. This explains, in part, the low percentages in Table 3.3.

Other coping strategies involved location decisions and hiring practices. A participant in Puebla (apparel) stated that his establishment had moved three times in the last year, in search of lower rent and more space (specifically for sewing machines), but chose to remain in the same neighbourhood so as not to increase employee travel time. Various participants indicated that they had toyed with the idea of moving, but later abandoned it, partly for fear of losing (already) trained workers. In sum, employee skill levels can affect establishment mobility, especially where public transportation is costly or deficient. A more common strategy, identified by various participants, is for the establishment, once located, to choose employees on the basis of their place of residence. An establishment in San Salvador (apparel) only hires employees living within a given perimeter around the plant. Finally, a strategy adopted by many maquiladoras, which reduces the cost of lateness and absenteeism, is to pay workers according to piecework rather than hours.

3. PUBLIC SAFETY AND SECURITY

Estimating the cost of inferior public security services was to some extent easier than that of other services. On the one hand, public security services involve significant direct costs (security guard wages, insurance premiums, payments to private security companies, etc.); on the other hand the issue of public security aroused considerable interest in all three cities. Local law enforcement services were considered woefully inadequate and the opinion of the local police was generally low. Nonetheless, the results (Table 3.4) must be interpreted with caution since they fail to fully account for indirect costs, and overlap with the results for transport services and regulatory and administrative conditions. The absence of estimates for San Salvador is a pity since, as we shall see in the next chapter, security concerns are more prevalent there than in Puebla and San José.

Table 3. 4: Estimated Impact of Inferior Service on Costs [% of Total Operating Cost]: Public Safety

Values	Puebla		San José	
	Apparel	Food Processing	Apparel	Food Processing
Mean	4.0	1.5	2.4	1.1
Median	5.0	1.5	2.3	1.3
Minimum	2.0	0.1	1.0	0.5
Maximum	5.0	2.5	4.0	1.5

The estimates on the impact of public safety range from a minimum of 0.1% of total costs to a maximum of 5%, with means and medians between 1.1% and 5%. In this case, the apparel industry in both Puebla and San José appear to be noticeably affected. In evaluating the costs related to poor public safety, it is useful to distinguish between the costs of protecting persons and those of protecting goods and property. The former are generally less quantifiable than the latter, partly because they involve the costs of perceived danger, stress and other psychological costs. The direct link with employee behaviour is not always easy to establish. The protection of property will generally entail direct outlays. For example, a firm in Puebla (food processing) had equipped itself with a sophisticated tracking system to electronically follow goods as they move from the plant to customers or between plants. The plant appeared to have considerable success in reducing theft and loss. However, as was equally pointed out, such equipment is beyond the means of all but the largest firms.

The most common coping strategy was to hire security guards to accompany trucks or to subcontract deliveries to private security companies. The stretch between Puebla and Mexico City appears to be especially problematic; one participant indicated that he had recently lost an entire shipment (truck) on the way to Mexico City, undoubtedly stolen. Horror stories abound. However, the most crucial concern involved the transport of money. In addition to the need for security personnel, especially during deposits, some establishments have imposed more frequent stops (to deposit money) in order to minimize the amount carried at any given time. This, however, translated into increased driving time and extra driver pay. The dangers and costs involved in handling money also spill over into the protection of persons. For the majority of establishments, payday is a veritable nightmare. In each discussion group, there was at least one story of a participant (or one of his employees) having been attacked on payday as he (or she) left the building. Employees are generally paid in cash. A Puebla firm (food processing) hires private security guards to ensure that its employees are not mugged as they leave the establishment. Another establishment (also in Puebla) attempted to circumvent the problem by introducing direct bank deposits. However, this solution was rejected by employees, given the high service charges imposed by the bank, a revealing example of the (far from obvious) link between local public security and an efficient banking system.

Costs linked to personal security play out at various levels. Many workers (especially female) simply refuse to work night shifts. Where it is possible to convince employees to work night shifts (or other odd hours), coping mechanisms tie in with those previously mentioned for public transportation: extra compensation, rest areas, as well as the hiring of other personnel (including medical services) to ensure adequate working conditions. Kidnappings (of managers and executives) was a concern expressed in all three cities. This, in turn, affects the travel patterns of managers, as well as personal security expenses, for example, the purchase of bulletproof vehicles or personal guards. Public safety risks (to both persons and property) have led one San Salvador firm to hire recognized delinquents, familiar with the terrain, to guide its vehicles through the most dangerous barrios. Examples of imaginative adaptation are as varied as the particular circumstances, but none are without cost, even if these could not always be measured.

As noted earlier, participants generally manifested a high level of mistrust towards local officialdom, not least the police. In many cases, it was felt that the costs related to reporting crimes (especially thefts) outweighed the cost of the crimes themselves. By the same token, some expressed the opinion that it was less costly to accept the loss of a shipment than to report it to the insurance company and pay higher premiums, which, in any case, would have little positive effect on the security of property or personnel. All establishments had insurance coverage against theft and property damage, but it was generally felt to be a formality, a requirement rather than a significant cost-saving device. Reporting the crime to local authorities was often perceived as involving additional costs, not only in terms of paperwork and interminable meetings with officials, but also bribes to help get things done. Even then, a profitable outcome (goods recovered) was far from a foregone conclusion. In some cases, it was even suggested that the police were working with local felons (or at least were aware of their identity), an incentive to bribery (to keep their "accomplices" at bay), and to non-reporting. The general level of disenchantment with local law enforcement may explain the philosophical attitude of managers, and thus their inclination to downplay the true cost, since it is one they have so little control over.

4. BASIC URBAN SERVICES

Basic urban services refer to water and sanitation, power, and solid waste collection and disposal. According to the results (Table 3.5), the cost of not having adequate urban services is larger in Puebla than in San José. Establishments in the apparel industry in Puebla are heavy users of water. Technologies in the apparel industry, where fabrics sometimes need to go through various cycles of washing and dying, require an extensive supply of water. It is also useful to recall that Puebla is located in a relatively dry region in Mexico's central Meseta. Even once this has been taken into account, the percentages remain lower than might otherwise be expected, certainly when compared to the results obtained for the other classes of services. The results range from a low of 0% to a high of 5%, with means and medians between 0.8% and 2.4%. In sum, once put into perspective, the costs attributed to the malfunctioning of these traditional "hard" public services appear fairly small.

Table 3.5: Estimated Impact of Inferior Service on Costs [% of Total Operating Cost]: Basic Urban Services

Values	Puebla		San José	
	Apparel	Food Processing	Apparel	Food Processing
Mean	7.0	0.8	1.6	2.4
Median	1.0	1.0	0.8	1.8
Minimum	0.0	0.0	0.0	1.0
Maximum	20.0	1.5	5.0	5.0

This is not to say that there were no complaints. The chief concern by far was the quality of water services. In the three cities, all participating establishments are connected to central water and drainage systems, pay their water fees, and do not complain about the level of water charges. Complaints concerned water failures, fluctuations in pressure, and water quality (for example, high salinity levels, which can damage machinery). Coping strategies were those mentioned in the literature: the purchase of water from private sources, the digging of bore holes and sink-wells. Let us recall that these are services for which private alternatives exist. A participant in Puebla had considered moving his establishment to a neighbourhood with better water services, but then changed his mind, given the cost of moving.

Some of the concerns voiced by the groups dealt with additional costs imposed by new environmental regulations, especially with respect to sanitation and wastewater treatment. New systems, which need to be installed, are often costly. However, these costs are not the reflection of inferior public services, but the consequence of regulations to limit negative externalities. On the issue of sanitation and wastewater treatment, several participants noted that the issue went beyond the borders of their establishment, something about which they could do little, but which, nevertheless, increased their costs. Neighbouring plants or residents often had inferior drainage systems, and surrounding residents did not necessarily fully respect environmental regulations. In such cases, i.e., for services with significant externalities, the complaint, in the end, was addressed in the local regulatory environment.

Opinions on the quality of solid waste collection services were mixed. Some appeared quite satisfied with the service provided by local authorities, while others were less so. Some also stated that it was partly a matter of "luck," given the sometimes-erratic nature of the service. Besides irregularity, the main problems were the quantity of solid waste that needed to be collected, and the frequency of pick-ups. The primary coping strategy was contracting-out private waste collection services (often in addition to paying the municipal service charges). Finally, it is useful to note that establishments located in duty-free zones (for the two Central American cities) or in industrial parks were much more satisfied with the quality of basic services than others. In San Salvador, the costs are, in some cases, covered by the state, an implicit subsidy.

5. NORMS AND REGULATIONS

Because the impacts of norms and regulations on production costs are almost entirely indirect and intangible, participants had great difficulty formulating cost estimates. Participants from San Salvador frankly said that they were unable to attach a cost figure to the hours lost due to administrative vexations and procedures, although these were significant. As was the case for public safety, the estimates in Table 3.6 (and, again, only for Puebla and San José) necessarily contain a large dose of subjectivity and perception. As for public safety, we again face an apparent contradiction between low estimates and the high level of dissatisfaction expressed. Indeed, if we discount (again) the extreme case of apparel in Puebla, the percentages are very low, from a low of 0% to a high of 5%, with medians and means between 0% and 2.3%. This clearly flies in the face of the (common) image of regions where corruption, administrative arbitrariness and general bungling impose high costs on firms.

The participants consistently reported excessive regulations, notably in Puebla and San José. The number of steps required to startup a business were excessive, and each involved a different office. Seemingly unrelated approvals are sometimes required, as in the case of land use permits in San José: approval is conditional upon the registration of workers in the national social security system. Participants mentioned cases of procedures held up (or permits revoked) because a particular permit was accepted at one level only, but refused at another, or because interpretations differed from one civil servant to another. In some cases, participants mentioned "negotiating" the charge (or fine) or, frankly, paying a bribe. A participant in Puebla mentioned having to pay fines for infractions he had not committed: inspectors demanded "financial compensation" because the municipality requires them to meet a weekly quota of fines collected. A participant from San Salvador indicated his establishment paid, on average, $1000 to $2000 per month in "fines."

Table 3.6: Estimated Impact of Inferior Service on Costs [% of Total Operating Cost]: Norms and Regulations

Values	Puebla		San José	
	Apparel	Food Processing	Apparel	Food Processing
Mean	11.0	0.5	0.3	2.3
Median	10.0	0.5	0.0	1.5
Minimum	3.0	0.0	0.0	1.0
Maximum	20.0	1.0	1.0	5.0

These games are proportionally more costly for small firms and constitute an additional startup cost. An establishment in San José indicated having on its payroll a full-time person to deal with local authorities in such matters as the payment of traffic fines and the filing of accident reports. In smaller firms, such tasks often fall to the plant manager and, sometimes, the owner. Firms in industrial parks and free trade zones (generally larger firms) were on the whole less perturbed by public administration. By the same token, it appears that exporting firms are less affected than those oriented towards local markets; the small local firms are most caught up in red tape. It appears that, as a result of increasing openness and export-orientation, all three nations (Mexico, El Salvador, Costa Rica), have made considerable progress in lightening the load for exporting firms. El Salvador has gone the furthest in establishing a *ventilla única* (one-stop window), with some success, to help exporters handle administrative procedures. In this respect, the primary concern was less with waiting-lines for permits and such, but rather with the limited capacity of local officials to deal with issues of international trade and commerce.

CONCLUSIONS

Three supplementary conclusions can be drawn from the discussion groups:

1. Measuring the "true" costs of inferior localized public services is difficult because such costs are indirect and intangible. Most local business persons do not consider them as costs; they consider them as given, about which they can do little. In any case, their local competitors face the same constraints.

2. Notwithstanding the previous point, the costs are not negligible. The inferior quality of localized public services in Puebla and San José adds about 10% to total operating costs or, by the same token, reduces potential revenues by the same amount (the combined mean and median vary between 8.5% and 12.7%). Basic urban services are only a minor consideration (cost factor) when added to other concerns. Traffic control and road conditions (transport of goods), norms and regulations and public security come out as primary concerns. Most of these services, let us recall, are "pure" public goods for which there are no private alternatives.

3. The services are strongly interconnected and interrelated. It is not always obvious where one begins and the other ends. This is especially the case with the links between transportation, public safety, and the local regulatory climate. The relationship between the quality of basic urban services and the regulatory framework is also clear[4]. As shown by the results in Table 3.7, issues of trust, honesty and consistency are important when considering the quality of localized public services. In this respect, the links between the local institutional culture and the broader national institutional culture need to be taken into account.

Table 3.7: Estimated Impact of Inferior Service on Costs [% of Total Operating Cost] Synthesis: Combined Results for both Cities

Values	Transport of Goods	Transport of Persons	Public Safety	Basic Urban Services	Norms & Regulations	Total
Apparel						
Mean	4.7	1.9	3.1	3.9	4.9	18.5
Median	4.0	1.0	2.5	1.0	1.0	9.5
Food Processing						
Mean	4.5	1.4	1.4	1.3	1.0	9.5
Median	4.0	1.0	1.5	1.0	1.0	8.5
Total						
Mean	4.6	1.6	2.0	2.2	2.4	12.7
Median	4.0	1.0	1.5	1.0	1.0	8.5

Notes

[1] See Appendix 2 for the discussion template applied at all meetings. Additional methodological issues are discussed in Chapter 2.

[2] An example of the link between public safety and transportation is the practice, in some neighbourhoods of San José, of not stopping at red lights after nightfall, a practice largely tolerated by local authorities.

[3] We use the term "public" transport as a synonym for the less elegant "collective" transport, but without inferring public sector ownership or operation.

[4] Recall that the two were amalgamated in our survey questionnaire (see Appendix 1).

CHAPTER 4

The Impact of Inferior Localized Public Services:
Survey Results

This chapter presents the results of a survey conducted in 165 establishments in five cities during the first months of 2002[1]. Most of the results presented are descriptive in nature due, again, to the small size of the samples. The problems encountered in administering the questionnaires are explained in greater detail in Chapter 2. Figure 4.1.1 gives an overview of the survey samples by urban area (city). Given the sample sizes per city and the variable quality of responses, results are, as a rule, most robust for Puebla and San José. It is generally for these two Southern cities that the questionnaire responses were the most complete and completed with the greatest care. Montreal respondents also filled out questionnaires with great care. The most serious problems arose in San Salvador and in Belo Horizonte, where the low level of trust and general unwillingness to share information (especially of a financial nature) led to low response rates and/or to incomplete questionnaires, often with ambiguous answers[2]. In Belo Horizonte, the food-processing sector simply refused to collaborate in the survey.

The results presented are limited to certain questions, where we feel sufficiently confident of the validity of responses. By the same token, the relative nature of many questions (and answers) needs to be stressed, especially for (non quantitative) questions requiring a judgment. For example, Montrealers, in the North, may well indicate that road congestion is an important problem simply because, compared to other problems (crime, corruption, road repair, failed urban services, etc.), this issue affects them most. In a Southern city, an "objective" traffic congestion problem may be just as bad, or worse, but will not be perceived as such, because it is a minor irritant compared to other problems. This needs to be kept in mind when interpreting our results. As we shall see, the differences in perception between the establishments surveyed in Southern cities and those in Montreal, our Northern point of comparison, are generally considerable, a sign that problems are indeed very different.

1. GENERAL ESTABLISHMENT CHARACTERISTICS BY CITY

In all figures, results for both sectors (apparel and food-processing) are aggregated[3], principally because of the small size of survey samples.

Establishment size, in terms of number of employees, varies between the five cities, with Belo Horizonte and San Salvador at the two extremes, the former with

Figure 4.1.1: Survey Sample: Number of Establishments by Sector and City

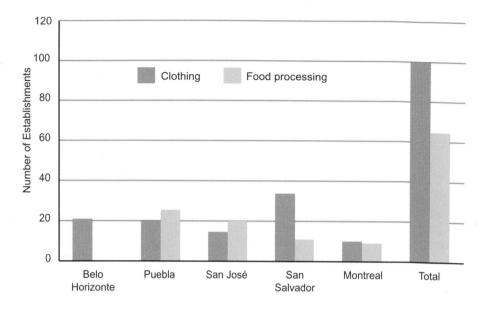

Figure 4.1.2: Employees per Establishment

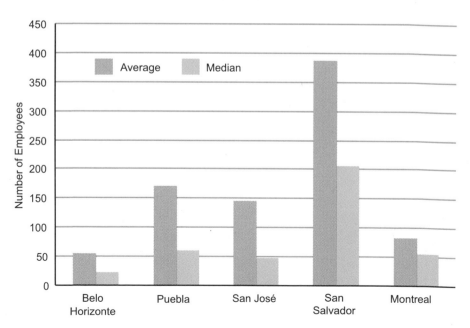

smallest number of establishments (Figure 4.1.2). This may help to explain why both average sales per establishment and average sales per employee are so low in Belo Horizonte (Figures 4.1.3 and 4.1.4). As would be expected, average sales figures (per establishment and per employee) are significantly higher in Montreal, which is a reflection of higher productivity levels.

The establishments surveyed in the five cities show comparable patterns on three fronts: (a) women in the workforce, (b) control, and (c) cost structures. Women (Figure 4.1.5) constitute a significant proportion of the workforce everywhere (with data missing for Belo Horizonte), which is not surprising given the industries surveyed: apparel and food industries are traditionally female labour intensive. In all five cities, establishments surveyed are overwhelmingly under local control (Figure 4.1.6). As noted in the previous chapter, locally controlled firms are generally more comfortable responding to a survey of this kind because of their greater identification with the community[4]. The similarity in cost structures is more surprising, suggesting that the basic technologies used (in the two industries) may not be that different between cities, although the absolute value of capital per worker is significantly higher in Montreal (Figure 4.1.7).

The results for market orientation are easy to interpret (Figure 4.1.8). As would be expected, San Salvador firms are the most export-oriented, a reflection both of their greater size and the small size of the host nation. The inverse holds true for Belo Horizonte: small firms in a city located at the centre of a huge national market, far from an international border. The export-orientation of Montreal-based establishments is a reflection of the general openness of the Canadian economy, although non-tariff barriers remain significant in the apparel industry. Larger firms are, as a rule, more export-oriented than smaller ones (Figure 4.1.9). Also, not surprisingly, smaller establishments are proportionally more concentrated in the central parts of urban areas (Figure 4.1.10).

The establishments surveyed display similar basic reasons for locating in the city (Figures 4.1.11 and 4.1.12). The weight of the "owner-founder lives here" variable is a useful reminder of the link between the performance of urban economies and their capacity to nurture successful startup businesses. In most business location surveys, the origins of the owner-founder generally come out as the first or second explanatory factor. Figure 4.1.13 in turn confirms, as would be expected, the link between the "owner-founder lives here" factor and size. Startups often begin in the central parts of the city as small family firms, and then move to the periphery as the need for floor space grows.

If we disregard the "owner-founder" factor, proximity is by far the overwhelming consideration: proximity to clients, to suppliers, and to complementary firms. In sum, the basic factors driving agglomeration noted in Chapter 1 continue to hold. Firms agglomerate to overcome the costs associated with distance. It is useful to recall that we are dealing here with two relatively low-tech industries, which largely explains why "proximity to a pool of skilled manpower scored relatively low. The type of skills required by these firms may be assumed to be fairly ubiquitous. Within the broad proximity factor, proximity to clients is clearly the chief driving force (Figure 4.1.12); this holds true for all four Southern cities, less so for Montreal. Notably, in the cases of Belo Horizonte and San José, the pull of the city is plainly

Figure 4.1.3: Average Sales per Establishment (US$ 2001)

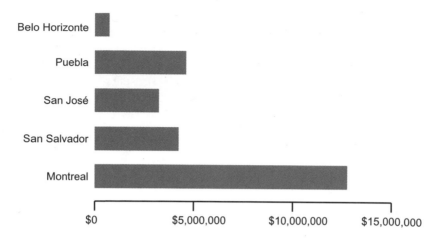

Figure 4.1.4: Average Sales per Employee (US$ 2001)

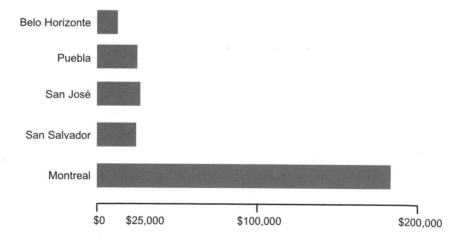

linked to its position as the centre of the local-regional market (see Figure 4.1.8). Centrality matters.

Figure 4.1.14 gives the annual worker turnover rates for different occupational classes (all cities). High turnover rates can constitute a major cost for firms, especially where training is an important factor. Even for relatively unskilled workers, training can constitute a not insignificant cost. If Figure 4.1.15 is to be believed, the average number of days needed to render an unskilled worker operational varies from a low of six days (Belo Horizonte) to a high of twenty-two in San Salvador. However, for skilled workers, the maximum values are generally in the range of thirty-plus days (for all three Hispanic cities), with a low of twelve days in Belo Horizonte[5]. Thus, the replacement of a skilled worker constitutes an important cost (in terms of foregone production during the training period).

As expected, the highest turnover rates are found among unskilled workers and the lowest among managerial and professional personnel, a reflection of the relative ease with which the establishments are willing to let go (and replace) particular employees. Unskilled workers are the least stable class in all cities except San Salvador (Figure 4.1.16). Most striking, however, is the discrepancy between Montreal and the four Southern cities in the data regarding office and sales personnel, and skilled workers. As a whole, turnover rates for these two occupational classes are significantly lower in Montreal, suggesting higher recruitment and training costs in the Southern cities, an indication that we are indeed dealing with very different urban environments. Differences in worker turnover rates can be attributed partly, we shall suggest, to differences in problems related to the movement of persons (commuting), and to safety and security.

Figure 4.1.5: Women as a % of all Employees

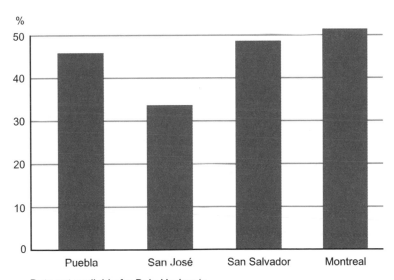

Data not available for Belo Horizonte

Figure 4.1.6: Establishments [%] Domestically Controlled*

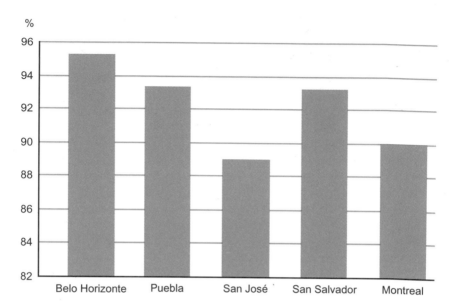

*Locally owned, head office, or subsidiary of a domestically controlled firm

Figure 4.1.7: Percentage Breakdown of Operating Costs

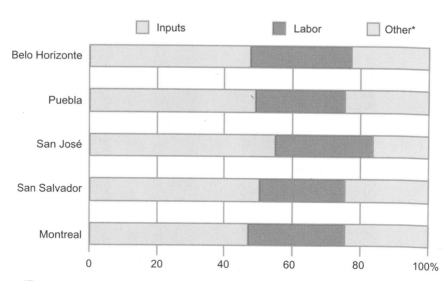

*Transport, taxes, rental costs, business services, other

Figure 4.1.8: Market Orientation by City. Percentage of Sales by Destination

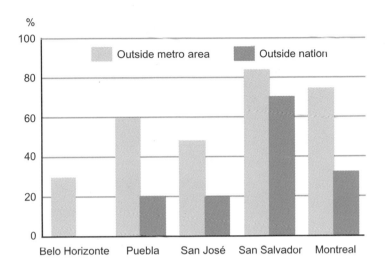

Figure 4.1.9: Market Orientation by Establishment Size

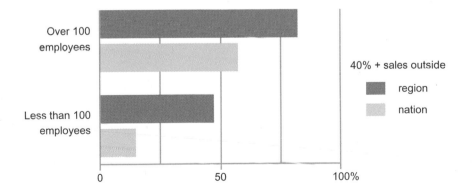

Figure 4.1.10: Location within Urban Region by Establishment Size

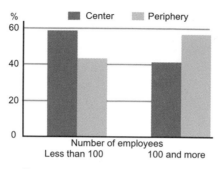

Data not available for Belo Horizonte

Figure 4.1.11: Factors Determining the Location of Establishment in the Metropolitan Area, All Cities*

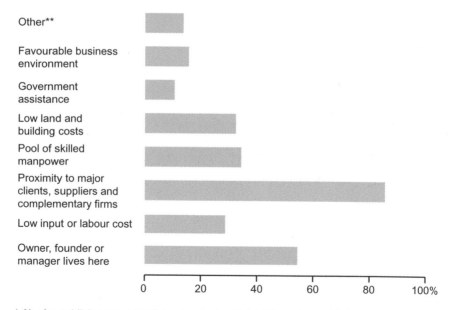

* % of establishments identifying the factor. Establishments could choose up to 3 factors.
** Includes low local taxes, better quality of life and "other"

Figure 4.1.12: Chief Factors Determining the Location of Establishment in the Metropolitan Area*

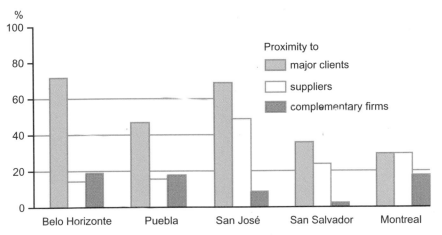

Breakdown of class "proximity to clients, suppliers and complementary firms" (figure 4.1.11)
* % of establishments identifying the factor. Establishments could choose up to 3 factors.

Figure 4.1.13: Respondents who Answered that "Owner, Founder or Manager Lives There" by Size of Establishment

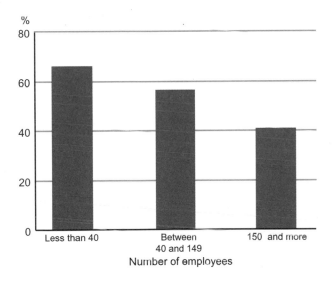

Figure 4.1.14: Annual Worker Turnover: Last Five Years, All Cities

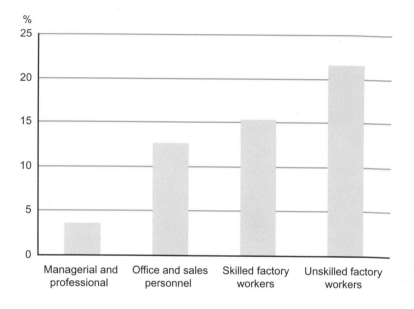

Figure 4.1.15: Average Days of Training by Occupation

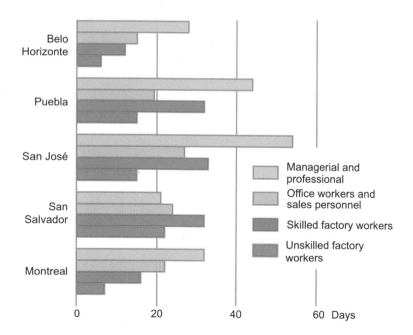

Figure 4.1.16: Annual Turnover by Occupation

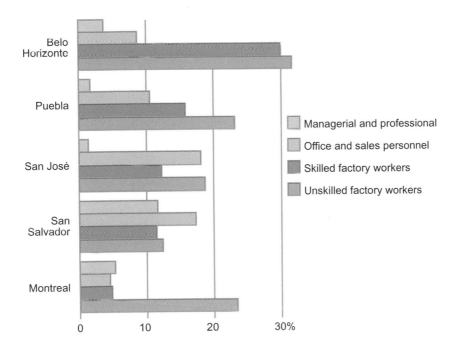

Figure 4.2.1: Estimated Impact (on Operating Costs) of Problems Related to Merchandise Transport

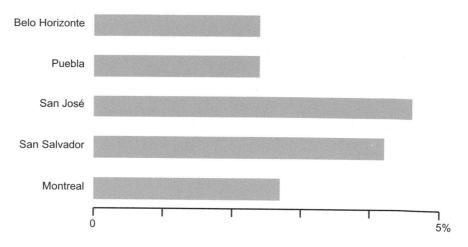

Figure 4.2.2: Establishments [%] Responding that Congestion Had an Impact on Costs

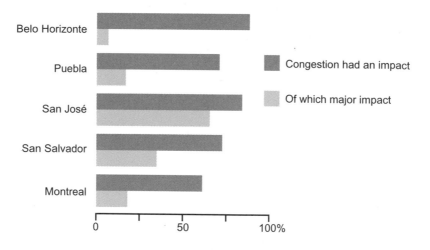

2. TRANSPORT (MERCHANDISE)

Figure 4.2.1 suggests that congestion costs were highest in San José and San Salvador. It is interesting to note that the chief difference is not between Montreal and Southern cities, but rather between the Southern cities themselves. Traffic conditions indeed appear to be much worse in San José and San Salvador (traffic management, road repair, etc.) than in Puebla and Montreal. It should be noted that the state government of Puebla has, in recent years, invested heavily in better traffic management, road maintenance, and road construction in the Puebla urban area (including the completion of a ring (loop) highway linking suburban industrial districts[6]). The results in Figure 4.2.1 appear to suggest that these investments have paid off.

Figure 4.2.2 suggests a more systematic difference between Montreal and Southern cities. Approximately 61% of establishments in Montreal indicated that congestion impacted costs, compared to 72% to 88% for Southern cities. Again, the costs appear most significant in San Salvador and San José for this variable (% major impact). The difference becomes more apparent in Figure 4.2.3, when the cost impact is related to poor road and street conditions (maintenance and repair). Establishments in the South have a greater tendency to attribute traffic-related costs to road maintenance problems than to congestion per se. Conditions were judged worse in the central parts of the city than in suburban locations, both in terms of congestion and road maintenance (Figures 4.2.4 to 4.2.6).

The difference between Montreal and the South (leaving aside Belo Horizonte) is most evident with respect to the frequency of late deliveries (Figure 4.2.7). The question behind Figure 4.2.7 is factual, with little room for personal judgment or misinterpretation. This suggests that cost estimates for Montreal in Figure 4.2.1 may be too high when compared to the others, since poor road conditions were perceived to have had only a minor cost impact in Montreal (see Figure 4.2.3) and since the chief impacts of traffic congestion are time lost and lateness[7]. The difference is further accentuated in Figure 4.2.8, where respondents were asked to indicate the chief impacts of lateness in deliveries to clients. With the exception of Montreal respondents, all others (in varying degrees) indicated that lateness prevented them from developing new markets. In other words, firms are at a comparative disadvantage for serving markets where timely deliveries are an essential component of the product. This is not an insignificant factor in industries where just-in-time production and distribution methods are important.

Figure 4.2.3: Establishments [%] Responding that Poor Road & Street Conditions Impacted Production Costs

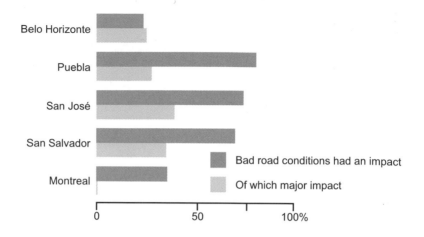

Figure 4.2.4: Estimated Impact (on Operating Costs) of Problems Related to Merchandise Transport, by Location Within Urban Area

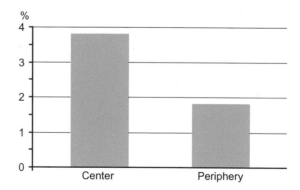

Figure 4.2.5: Establishments [%] Responding that Congestion Impacted Production Costs, by Location Within Urban Area, Southern Cities

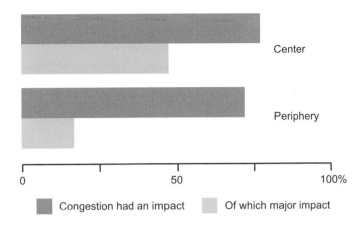

Figure 4.2.6: Establishments [%] Responding that Poor Road Conditions Impacted Production Costs, by Location Within Urban Area, Southern Cities

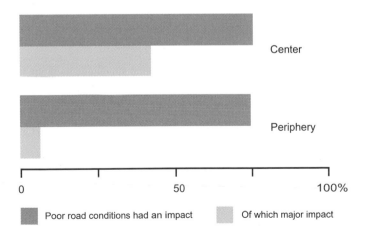

Figure 4.2.7: Establishments Responding that Deliveries Arrived Late at Least Once a Week

*Results for Belo Horizonte should be interpreted with caution

Figure 4.2.8: Impact of Lateness in Deliveries to Customers: % Distribution of Those Responding that this Occurred at Least Once

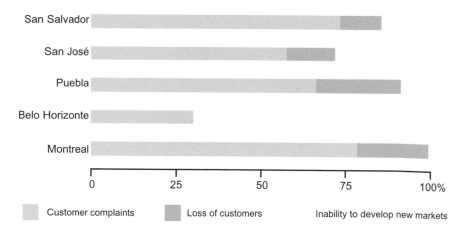

3. MOVEMENT OF PERSONS

The results in Figure 4.3.1 are in line with those from the Puebla and San José discussion groups, with regards to the perceived impacts on costs of inferior public transport systems. These impacts are seen as less significant than costs related to the transport of goods, probably because, as we suggested, a large portion of the costs are transferred to the employees themselves. However, the results for San Salvador and Belo Horizonte suggest that these costs can be significant, equal to or surpassing those attributed to poor merchandise transport services. The cost estimates in San Salvador and Belo Horizonte are probably related to the higher prevalence of problems with personal security and safety in these two cities (next section), a relationship that also came out during the discussion group meetings.

Particular caution must be used when making a comparison between the Southern results regarding this service and Montreal's. As would be expected, the means of transport used by employees vary considerably (Figure 4.3.2): approximately 56% of Montreal-based employees came to work by car, compared to a maximum of 14.2% in San José. Not surprisingly, the percentage was lowest (4.7%) in the poorest city, San Salvador. If we consider the time lost variable, i.e., lateness (Figure 4.3.3), the difference between Montreal and the other cities again becomes apparent. In both cases (goods and people), we may assume that the greater prevalence of lateness has a number of causes, among which traffic control and the ease of commuting may not be the only ones. In sum, impediments to the movement of people and goods within cities are generally greater in the South.

A North-South difference may also be observed in the data regarding relative ease of personal interaction, i.e., possibilities for face-to-face contacts and business meetings (Figure 4.3.4). Missed business meetings are generally more frequent in the South. This also raises the issue of how different individuals (and societies) value the importance of time lost and, as a corollary, of opportunities lost. We cannot assume that all societies value time in the same way. The differing valuation of time is indirectly reflected in Figure 4.3.5. As expected, only a minority of Montreal respondents (31.3%) indicated that lost business meetings affected their productivity. However, meetings that were missed were considered of more importance than elsewhere. In other words, Montrealers lost fewer business meetings, but placed a higher value on those losses than citizens from the other cities surveyed. Looking at the Southern results, one might, for example, reasonably argue that the low value for Puebla (7.9% of meetings lost were considered to have had a major impact) reflects the relatively low value Mexicans put on time and, as corollary, the relatively little importance given to missed business meetings (or lateness). By the same token, it is difficult, when interpreting Figure 4.3.3, to disentangle the true effects of poor commuting services from those of culture and social values. The possible feedback effects between observed behaviour and cultural values must be constantly kept in mind.

Cultural considerations aside, face-to-face contacts and business meetings are vital cogs in the wheel of an efficiently functioning city. Indeed, they are one of the fundamental economic reasons for the very existence of cities: Figure 4.3.6 confirms the importance of face-to-face business meetings. Fully 95% of all respondents

Figure 4.3.1: Estimated Impact (on Operating Costs) of Problems Related to the Movement of Persons

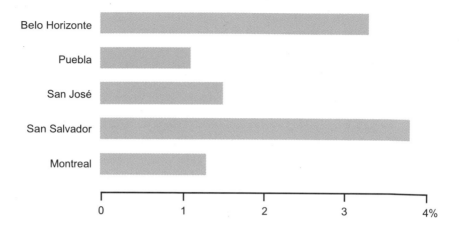

Figure 4.3.2: Means of Transport Used by Employees

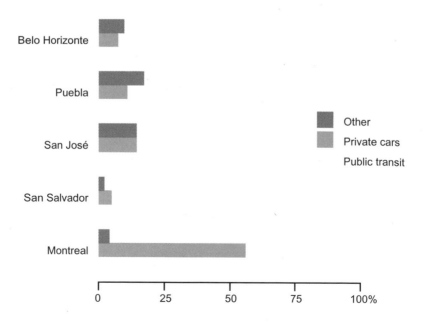

considered it important (of which 82%, very important) to meet with clients at least once a month. The percentage is over 70% for all classes: suppliers, bankers, consultants, etc. Respondents in Southern cities generally seemed to grant business meetings a higher level of importance than those in Montreal (Figures 4.3.7 and 4.3.8). Here again, cultural and institutional factors may come into play. Personal relationships may be considered more important in Southern Latin cultures or, as a corollary, the generally lower level of trust means that personal contacts are even more essential for business transactions. In institutional environments where rules are less clear, transaction costs will be higher and, correspondingly, so will the need to meet. Especially revealing is the difference in Montreal's data for contacts with consultants, bankers, or other financial advisers (Figure 4.3.8). Once again, it can be argued that this is a reflection of the South's less efficient financial systems and unclear rules, (requiring more frequent personal encounters) and/or lower levels of trust, where financial transactions absolutely require face-to-face meetings[8]. Whatever the explanation, the implications are the same: the existence of an urban environment where interaction is facilitated is no less important in the South than in the North.

Figure 4.3.9 lends credence to the hypothesis that trust (or, rather, lack of it) explains the greater importance of face-to-face meetings. Belo Horizonte and San Salvador are, arguably, the two most "conflict-ridden" and unsafe cities sampled (see next section). Face-to-face meetings are essential for business transactions in these cities (at least, more so than in the others) and, as such, missed occasions have a high cost. In economic terms, transaction costs are highest in these cities. One of the results of this situation would appear to be a much greater reliance in these cultures on informal networks, especially family relations. The link with dysfunction in formal financial systems is not difficult to make.

Figure 4.3.10 reveals an additional difference. In gauging the impact of missed meetings, Southern respondents tended to give a greater weight to lost opportunities and lost information (once again, more so in Belo Horizonte and San Salvador). These results suggest not only higher transaction costs, but also higher information costs in general. Without wishing to stretch the point too far, it could be argued that this, in turn, affects relative rates of innovation and investment in new production techniques.

Figure 4.3.3: Establishments [%] Responding that Employees Arrived Late at Least Once a Week Causing Production Losses

*Results for Belo Horizonte should be interpreted with caution

Figure 4.3.4: Respondents [%] who Missed at Least One Business Meeting a Month Due to Poor Traffic Conditions

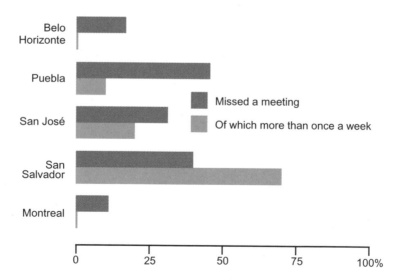

Figure 4.3.5: Establishments [%] Responding that Missed Business Meetings Had Impacted their Productivity

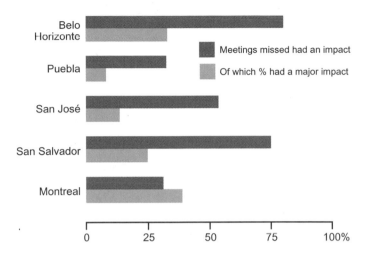

Figure 4.3.6: Respondents [%] Indicating that it is Important to Meet the Following Persons at Least Once a Month, All Cities

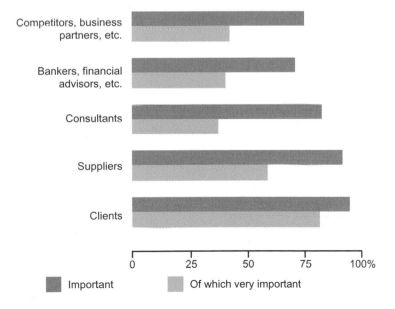

Figure 4.3.7: Respondents [%] Indicating that it is Very Important for them to Meet at Least Once a Month with Clients or Suppliers

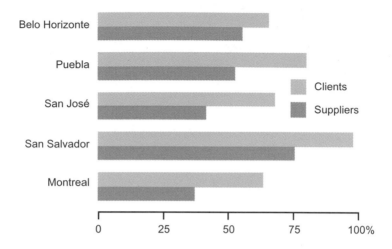

Figure 4.3.8: Respondents [%] Indicating that it is Very Important to Meet at Least Once a Month with Bankers or Consultants

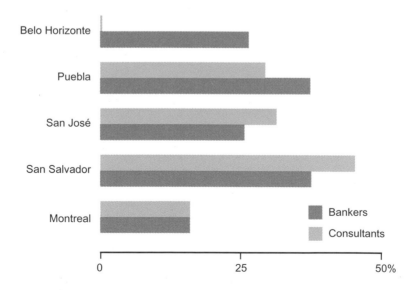

Figure 4.3.9: Composite Index of the Impact of Lost Business Meetings*

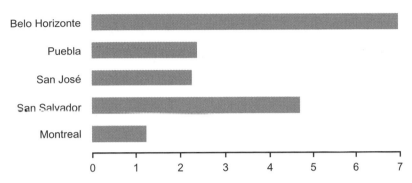

*Respondants could check 4 possible impacts (see figure 4.3.10) giving their importance ("none[0]","some[1]","major[2]"). The index constitutes the weighted sum of responses.

Figure 4.3.10: Relative Weight of Possible Impacts of Lost Business Meetings*

*Distribution of totals on figure 4.3.9

Figure 4.4.1: Estimated Impact (on Operating Costs) of Problems Related to Security and Protection: Per City

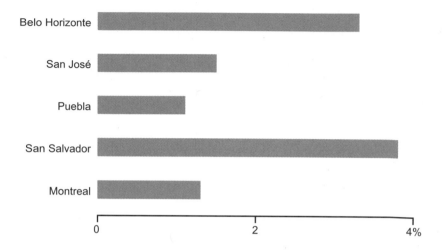

Figure 4.4.2: Security Related Personnel as a % of Total Workforce

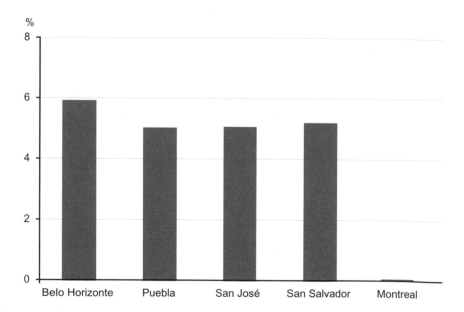

4. SECURITY AND PUBLIC SAFETY

Once again, we see the impact of relative perceptions and evaluations in the data on security and public safety. Not surprisingly, costs resulting from problems of security and public safety are rated highest in San Salvador and Belo Horizonte (Figure 4.4.1), arguably among the least safe cities in the Americas. But, since living with crime may, in such cases, have become a way of life, so to speak, respondents may not always be aware of the extra costs that urban crime imposes on their establishments. This becomes apparent when we compare the results of Figure 4.4.1 with those of Figure 4.4.2. On this basis of this comparison alone, one might argue that safety and security problems add at least 5% to the cost of wages in Southern cities, as compared to Montreal. However, it is possible that many Southern respondents consider this a "normal" cost, and thus do not make the link with the question whose responses are illustrated by Figure 4.4.1. Having a security guard at the front door is so commonplace that it is simply no longer seen as an abnormal expenditure.

The costs of crime and urban violence go beyond direct financial impacts, as was made clear in the discussion groups. Figure 4.4.3 illustrates the range of possible impacts. Significantly, although evaluations vary greatly between categories, none of the possible impacts received a zero answer. In other words, urban crime problems were perceived, in varying degrees, to impact a broad spectrum of factors affecting business operations. Some 30% of surveyed establishments indicated that crime affected their ability to operate at full capacity. As illustrated by Figure 4.4.4, this impact is considered greatest in Southern cities. The impact is undoubtedly largely indirect, partly due to the effects of crime on employee safety and, as a corollary, the ability and willingness of employees to work at different times of the day.

In this respect, perhaps the most interesting result concerns the differential impact of urban crime on the hiring and retention of male and female workers, a point also raised during the discussion groups. This impact is significantly greater for female than for male workers. Indeed, in relative terms, the impact on the hiring of women comes out as the most important impact of urban crime. This is the case for all Southern cities, except San José, where the impact is given equal weight with the impact on the ability to operate at full capacity (Figure 4.4.4). It is not difficult to make the link between female hiring, high turnover rates (see Figure 4.1.16) and the inability to operate at full capacity. As was noted during the group discussions, crime or deficient and unsafe public transportation, which make it difficult to attract (and hold) women workers, can constitute obstacles to the introduction of evening and night shifts.

The nature of crime also differs between Montreal and the Southern cities (Figures 4.4.5 and 4.4.6). Theft is a common occurrence everywhere (Figure 4.4.5), although less so in Montreal, as might be expected. What really distinguishes Montreal from the other cities is the level of violent crime (Figure 4.4.6). As might be expected, Belo Horizonte and San Salvador appear to be the least secure places to do business. Some 58% of San Salvador firms responded that assaults with a weapon occurred on their premises approximately once a month (26%, once a week), which is frightening by any standard. The results are no less reassuring for

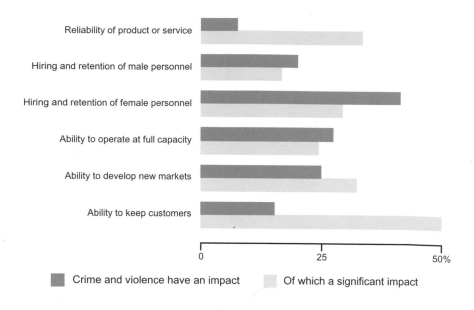

Figure 4.4.3: How Crime and Violence Impact Establishments: % Identifying Impact, All Cities

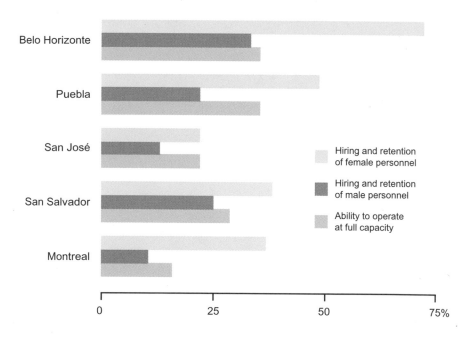

Figure 4.4.4: Chief Impacts of Crime and Violence on Establishments by City: % Identifying Impact

Belo Horizonte; assaults with weapons occurred near the premises approximately once a month for 65% of establishments (25%, once a week). The results for Puebla also indicate a high risk of aggression near the premises (43% approximately once a month); these bring to mind the comments made during the discussion groups about the risks involved with payday. It is little wonder that women, especially, fear working under such conditions.

The results in Figure 4.4.5 suggest that one of the indirect effects of urban violence on economic growth may be the added costs imposed on the development of industries relying on a predominantly female labour force. Since the emergence of an apparel industry (and, at a later stage, electronics) is often the classical development path followed by developing nations (the case in much of eastern and southern Asia), urban crime can constitute a major handicap for nations that would "normally" have taken this path. Without wishing to overstate our case, the higher prevalence of urban crime in Latin American cities in general may explain, in part, why that continent has been less successful overall in developing vibrant apparel and electronics export sectors (with the exception of some maquiladora enclaves[9]).

The difference between North and South, and between safer and less-safe cities is also apparent in the different causes attributed to higher crime. Overall, inadequate police protection is, by far, seen as the dominant factor (Figure 4.4.7). However, it is of minor importance in Montreal (Figure 4.4.8). Therefore, it would seem that safer cities are also cities where crime is less likely to be attributed to inadequate police protection.

Figure 4.4.5: Theft of Merchandise or Money: Frequency of Occurrence

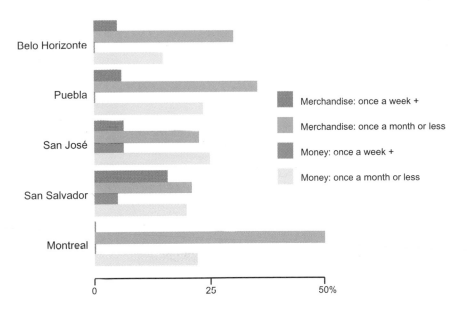

Figure 4.4.6: Assault with a Weapon: Frequency of Occurrence

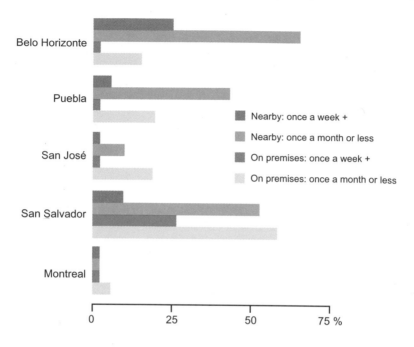

Figure 4.4.7: Factors that Contribute to Criminal Activity in the Neighbourhood: % Identifying Impact, All Cities

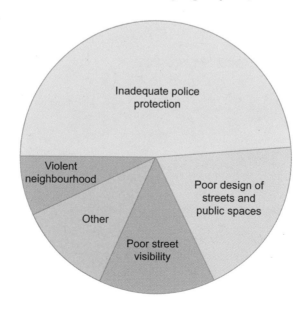

Figure 4.4.8: Inadequate Police Protection as a Factor Contributing to Criminal Activity in the Neighbourhood

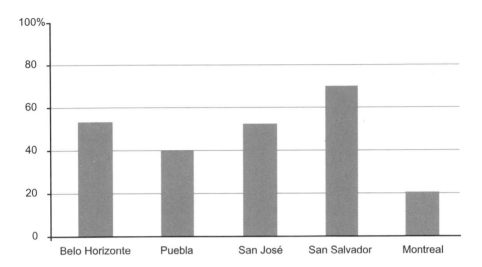

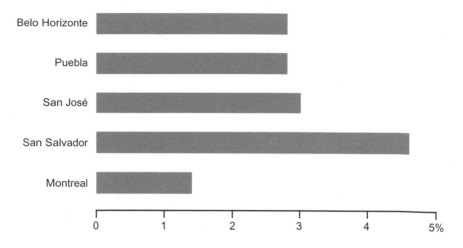

Figure 4.5.1: Estimated Impact (on Operating Costs) of Problems Related to the Local Regulatory Environment

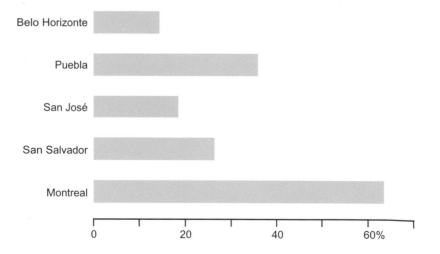

Figure 4.5.2: Establishments [%] that Feel Secure (Not Vulnerable to Arbitrary Administrative Decisions)

5. NORMS AND REGULATORY ENVIRONMENT

Questions related to the local regulatory environment once again reveal significant differences between North and South. If Figure 4.5.1 is to be believed, Montreal differs from the other cities because it does not share the latter's perception of the inadequacy (with the associated costs) of the local regulatory environment. This includes elements such as the trustworthiness and efficiency of the local bureaucracy and local officials. This is further brought home by the results of Figure 4.5.2, which shows that the majority of Montreal establishments (63%) felt themselves to be secure, i.e., not susceptible to arbitrary policy decisions or administrative fiat, compared, for example, to about 18% in San José and 14% in Belo Horizonte. It is not difficult to imagine the probable impact on the investments decisions and long-range planning of businesses, or the indirect impacts on risk evaluation and the cost of capital.

In sum, much of the differences are related to the overall institutional environment in the various cities, where considerations of public order, traffic safety, honesty, and general civility all overlap to create a distinct urban culture. Perhaps, for lack of a better term, this is best summed up in the expression "civic culture." However, creating a civic culture that can reap maximum gains from agglomeration is by no means a simple proposition.

6. CONCLUSIONS

Despite the risks of "relativity" and "subjectivity" implicit in the cost evaluation questions, the composite results are close to what would be predicted on the basis on the anecdotal evidence from the discussion groups (Figure 4.6.1). Composite cost evaluations, due to inferior local public services, are lowest in Montreal and highest in San Salvador, which is located in the poorest nation of the sample. Once a city like San Salvador (for which, let us recall, focus group estimates were unavailable) is introduced, the possible ceiling for the composite cost estimates of deficient localized services rises considerably, and may well be in the order of 20% for comparable cities. Accepting that all estimates are probably too low (especially in the South), the relatively lower estimates for San José and Puebla (with the latter coming out notably well) are also consistent with the literature and anecdotal information. Puebla, on the whole, gives the impression of a safe and well-run city, especially when compared with its three Southern counterparts.

It also not entirely surprising that, in relative terms, security concerns carry less weight in Puebla and San José than elsewhere (Figure 4.6.2). At the risk of overgeneralizing, more prosperous cities (i.e., located in nations with higher GDPs) would appear to be relatively more preoccupied with traffic problems, especially congestion, than with the transport of goods. However, Puebla's fairly good showing on this factor[10], as well as on the security variable, undoubtedly explains why the relative weight of the regulatory environment variable is highest there. Indeed, bureaucratic ineptitude, tinged with minor corruption, is what Poblanos are most likely to complain about, just as Belo Horizonte's inhabitants are more likely to gripe about crime and urban violence (not forgetting the link with public

Figure 4.6.1: Composite Estimated Impact of Inferior Localized Public Services

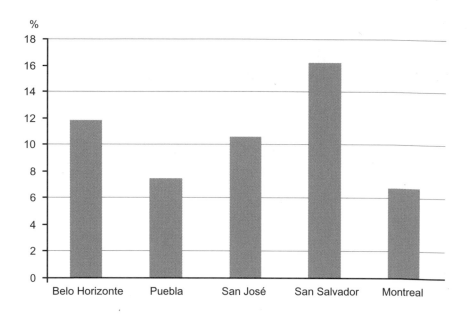

Figure 4.6.2: Distribution of Estimated Impact of Inferior Services Among Four Classes of Services*

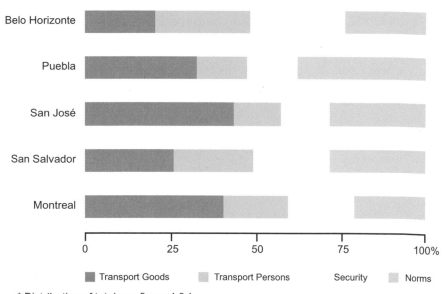

* Distribution of totals on figure 4.6.1

transportation). As noted at the outset, such cost evaluations are necessarily relative. Relative differences and perceptions not withstanding, the composite impact of deficient localized public services on productivity can be significant. If the 10% to 20% range is anywhere close to reality, deficient localized services can place a considerable burden on local firms.

On a more general level, the indirect, often hidden, effects of inferior localized public services can significantly impact the interaction potential of cities, as we have seen in both this and the previous chapters. The link with (the power of) agglomeration economies is not difficult to infer. The effects often overlap, are interrelated, and play out at various levels: recruitment costs, training costs, information and transaction costs, time lost, foregone meetings, flexibility lost, higher business startup costs, etc. It should come as no surprise that issues of security and ease of movement within the city keep reappearing. That, in the end, is what a city is all about, at least from an economic perspective: a place where people can safely interact to trade, exchange information, learn, and work. Cities will not fulfill their full potential as sources of economic growth where it is difficult and costly to interact. The full range of impacts is summarized in the general conclusion (see summary of major conclusions below).

Notes

[1]   The questionnaire can be found in Appendix 1.

[2]   In this respect, recall the low turnout for the discussion group meetings (previous chapter) in San Salvador, and the inability to organize any at all in Belo Horizonte. In the latter case, those approached clearly stated their reservations about participating in such discussion groups, where they might be asked "embarrassing" questions.

[3]   Recall that the results for Belo Horizonte only cover the apparel sector.

[4]   There is, however, no rigorous manner to verify the bias, if any, that this may have introduced, both because of the very small number of local firms and because ownership data is not always readily available for non-respondents.

[5]   This result suggests that the establishments surveyed in Belo Horizonte are generally very low-tech, an additional factor that, when added to small size, might explain the very low revenue figures (recall Figure 4.1.4).

[6]   The introduction of female police officers to direct traffic, notably in the center, also appears to have had a salutary effect.

[7]   Other possible costs include higher fuel and driver costs.

[8]   The "0%" result for bankers for Belo Horizonte (Figure 4.3.8) is, it appears, the reflection of a highly dysfunctional financial sector. Businesses, especially small businesses, simply do not trust banks, and thus have little contact with them. Commercial loans are rare. The memory of high inflation has left its mark.

[9]   Similar reasoning may be applied to conservative Islamic regimes that discourage women from working, although the origins of the obstacles to the hiring of female workers are, of course, different.

[10]   Recall our comments on Puebla's recent investment in transportation.

Summary of Major Conclusions and Findings

1. OVERVIEW: CITIES, URBANIZATION AND ECONOMIC DEVELOPMENT

The study begins by reviewing the relationship between cities and national economic development, asking, in essence, why cities in developing nations do not create more wealth. The strong relationship between levels of urbanization and levels of development (as measured by GDP per capita) is irrefutable, and has been confirmed time and again by numerous studies. However, there is debate on whether urbanization (city creation) per se promotes development, or whether urbanization, like many other adjustments, is a reaction to rising levels of development.

The ability of cities (defined as places rather than political jurisdictions) to create wealth rests in large part on what economists call "agglomeration economies"; that is, the productivity gains derived from the geographic concentration (in urban places) of industries and people. Agglomeration economies encompass a very broad range of factors (whose mix can change over time) that contribute to productivity gains: shared infrastructure costs, reduced labour recruitment costs, reduced transport costs, reduced interaction costs, scale economies due to local market size, knowledge spillovers, etc. The essence of the gains derived from agglomeration rests, so to speak, on the ability of economic agents to physically come together to "productively" interact.

The "productive" city thus incorporates a suitable national institutional environment that facilitates "productive" interaction: the rule of law, property rights, appropriate macroeconomic policies, etc. The evidence suggests that national attributes (cultural, institutional, political, etc.) remain the primary factors underlying the wealth-generation potential of cities. The pure gains from agglomeration will rapidly peter out in the absence of appropriate public sector involvement. We suggest that the national public policy environment will (given current technology) largely set the upper limits of potential agglomeration economies at any given moment in time.

How important then are local factors, recognizing that the frontier between what is local and what is national (or regional) is, by no means, clear-cut. This study focuses on the so-called "localized public services." We choose the term "localized" (rather than "local") to indicate that the service need not necessarily be provided by local administrations or authorities. The level of government that should provide the service is not at issue in this study. The essential point is that the service must necessarily be provided and consumed locally; it cannot be traded. And no imported substitutes are available. If traffic congestion imposes a cost, local firms cannot avoid this cost by purchasing (or importing) a substitute. Nor do private alternatives exist. The study looks at "pure" localized public services, that is, services for which, precisely, there are no obvious private alternatives. These services can only be provided through public financing, thus, the importance of the links with the overall prevailing institutional climate.

Much has been written on the private costs of failed (local) public services for which private alternatives exist: power generation, water, solid waste collection and disposal, etc. (see, notably, the work by K. S. Lee and his colleagues, cited in Chapter 1). By the same token, much has been written on the impact of "hard" infrastructure on development (roads, dams, harbours, etc.). However, little has been written on the costs to firms of inferior "pure" localized public services, specifically "softer" services relating to management, planning and delivery, partly because the relationships are difficult to quantify. That, in part, is the gap that this study seeks to fill.

The study focuses on services that a priori are most obviously related to the city's ability to effectively generate agglomeration economies (see below). Agglomeration economies, if they are to be fully realized, depend on services that facilitate interaction within the city, especially those relating to the movement of goods and people, and the efficient flow of information. Inferior services will, we suggest, increase the costs of interaction within the city. When such services fail, the potential for wealth creation in cities is reduced; that is the common thread running throughout this study.

2. THE STUDY: THE IMPACT OF INFERIOR LOCALIZED PUBLIC SERVICES

The study examined the impact of inferior localized public services on the performance of firms in five cities. In total, 165 business establishments in the apparel and food-processing industries were surveyed in Montreal (Canada), Belo Horizonte (Brazil), Puebla (Mexico), San José (Costa Rica), San Salvador (El Salvador). In all cases, the "city" was defined as the urbanized metropolitan area. The survey was complemented by six discussion group meetings with business persons (for the same industries) in the three Spanish-speaking cities.

The services examined were:

- The transport of goods within the city: traffic management and control, road and street maintenance, road safety, street design and planning.

- The movement of persons within the city: regulation and planning of public transportation (also, some overlap with the previous service).

- Public order and safety: mainly policing.

- The local regulatory environment with respect to basic urban services (water, sanitation, waste disposal, environmental safety, etc.): transparency, efficiency, enforcement of by-laws, permits.

As suggested above, these services most directly affect the ability of firms and individuals to interact "productively" (to trade goods, to commute and to communicate). This, in turn, impacts the scope and magnitude of agglomeration economies.

The impacts on firms of inferior services are often indirect, hidden and, as such, difficult to measure. These impacts are true (negative) externalities. Many costs are economic, not financial. Respondents did not easily grasp the concept of economic cost, making it difficult to attribute costs. Also, the effects of deficiencies in different services often overlap, intertwine, and reinforce each other. Thus, for example, poor traffic management and urban insecurity (crime) are not necessarily independent events.

Because of the indirect nature of many of the impacts, quantitative results must be treated with caution. In many cases, since there was no alternative to the cost imposed (by inferior services), respondents did not see the "true" additional cost, especially when the cost was also borne by all competitors within the city. A good example is the cost of private security guards, a universal practice in almost all Latin American cities and, thus, not perceived as an extra cost resulting from inferior public services. This also means that "true" costs were often underestimated. The discussion group exercise allowed us to better understand and interpret the (quantitative) survey results.

3. FINDINGS

Given these words of caution, our major findings are summarized below. Because of the often rough nature of our quantitative findings, but also because of our relatively small survey samples, we have chosen to show only selected results to illustrate particular points. The conclusions, listed below, are drawn both from the survey results and the qualitative information from the discussion groups with local business persons.

1. Urban crime, poor traffic management, and poor street and road conditions *reduce the potential for interaction and business meetings.* This, in turn, reduces the potential for information sharing, learning, and what economists call "knowledge spillovers," with possible long-range negative effects on the rate of innovation. Some 40% of respondents in San Salvador indicated they missed at least one meeting a month, of which 70%, more than once a week; 75% indicated that missed meetings negatively impacted productivity.

2. After lost time, Southern respondents considered the chief impacts of missed meetings to be lost opportunities and lost information. The reduced potential for meetings also *raises transaction costs,* especially in Latin cultures where the level of interpersonal trust (or what is also called "social capital") is low, and where face-to-face contacts are an essential element of business transactions. This, in turn, translates into a greater reliance on informal networks, often based on family ties and personal relationships. The need for meetings increases, we suggest, in situations where formal rules are unclear as does the importance of services that facilitate interaction within cities.

3. Poor traffic management, and street and road conditions, as well as poorly regulated collective transportation, *increase employee lateness.* Some 50% of San José respondents indicated that employees arrived late at least once a week, causing production slowdowns or stoppages. Part of the problem (specifically in San José) is related to poor street planning and design. It was also suggested that municipal fragmentation has negatively affected transportation planning and management, both as related to persons and goods (next point).

4. Poor traffic management, poor street and road maintenance, and urban crime *make timely deliveries more difficult.* Approximately 1/3 of San José respondents indicated that deliveries arrived late at least once a week. In all Southern cities, respondents indicated that (unlike the situation in Montreal) unpredictability reduced their ability to expand into markets where timely deliveries were required. This puts Southern cities at a disadvantage for products where just-in-time and analogous practices are an integral part of the production and marketing processes.

5. Urban crime and poor traffic management reduce the ability of firms to attract and retain employees, which translates into *higher recruitment and training costs.* Annual turnover rates for skilled factory workers were, on average, two-to-six times higher in Southern cities than in Montreal. On average, the training period for skilled factory workers was about 30 days in the three Spanish-speaking cities.

6. Urban crime, specifically violent crime, *reduces the ability of businesses to attract and retain female employees.* In all cities, this was identified as the chief impact of urban crime on firms. In Belo Horizonte, arguably the most violent city in our sample, 72% of the firms sampled identified this impact. This puts Southern cities at a disadvantage, especially for industries where access to a female labour force is essential.

7. Urban crime *reduces the enterprise's ability to operate at full capacity.* This was generally identified as the second most important impact. This is, in part, an indirect consequence of the previously identified impact. In unsafe cities, workers, especially women workers, will be less inclined to work night shifts or during odd hours.

8. Poor collective transportation, specifically infrequent service in the evening and at night, further exacerbates the crime's impact on a firm's ability to hire women and, in turn, to operate at full capacity. Here again, poor street design and poor lighting will add to the problem.

9. Urban crime *increases personnel costs.* On average, security personnel accounted for approximately 5% of total employed personnel in Southern cities, compared to 0% in Montreal. The discussion group exercise also revealed a (surprising) link between the functioning of the local banking

system, urban crime and security costs. Since banks are not trusted (or perceived to impose exorbitant service charges), employees are paid in cash, making payday a particularly hazardous occasion. The dependence on cash also increases the risks (and costs) of deliveries and pick-ups, requiring security guards on board.

10. A substandard local regulatory environment (i.e. enforcement of local by-laws, inspections, issuance of permits, etc.) *amplifies the perceived insecurity and vulnerability of firms*, and thus, indirectly, their risk assessment. In all Southern cities (and contrary to Montreal), the vast majority of firms surveyed (as many as 85% in Belo Horizonte) felt themselves vulnerable to arbitrary decisions by local officials or inspectors.

11. Our findings reinforce Lee's conclusion that inferior public services proportionally hit small firms the hardest, with a predictable impact on potential startup businesses and entrepreneurship. We found that small family-owned establishments are more often located in the older central parts of the city and are generally more dependent on local markets. Much of the efforts to streamline local public services are aimed at larger export-oriented firms, often located in industrial parks or duty-free zones. San Salvador is a case in point.

12. A substandard local regulatory environment, characterized by influence-peddling may partly result from the behaviour of private actors, which again puts smaller firms at a disadvantage. This is not only because larger firms have greater resources to "influence" officials and affect decisions, but also because such behaviour reinforces the general climate of insecurity and vulnerability.

13. A corollary of the above points is the reduction in private investment and local startup businesses, although the magnitude of this impact is impossible to measure. We cannot quantify the foregone investments, or the businesses that were never created. The negative effects will be most significant for industries dependant on information-sharing (knowledge spillovers), industries with high transaction costs, industries that require timely deliveries, and industries highly dependant on female labour.

14. The overall impact of inferior localized public services (i.e., those identified in the study) on costs was estimated to be in the 10% to 20% range, with the highest percentages in the two least "secure" cities: San Salvador and Belo Horizonte. That is to say that inferior services increased operating costs of the establishments surveyed by some 10% to 20%. However, these estimates must be considered very rough approximations, given the problems of measurement and perception noted earlier.

15. As was suggested at the outset of this conclusion, the relative weight of inferior *localized* public services (i.e., those studied here) in explaining the

lower "productivity" of Southern cities is undoubtedly far less than that of national attributes. However, because they are inextricably linked with the public sector and with the broader institutional environment, they are part of the larger puzzle of trying to understand why some urban places are more productive than others.

4. AVENUES FOR FURTHER RESEARCH

- The links between obstacles to interaction, knowledge spillovers and innovation need to be further explored. If firms, especially knowledge-intensive firms, cluster in order to maximize the gains from interaction (including informal encounters), then cities where movement is more difficult (and less safe) may be at a comparative disadvantage for developing knowledge-intensive industries.

- By the same token, the links between obstacles to interaction and training and recruitment need to be further explored. Access to a skilled labour force is a primary factor guiding the location of knowledge-intensive industries. If access is imperfect because of crime or poor traffic management, then the city is at a further disadvantage for developing knowledge-intensive industries.

- The link between urban crime, unsafe commuting, and the ability to hire women needs to be further explored. Our results suggest that the link is significant. If so, cities with high levels of violent crime are at a comparative disadvantage for developing industries dependent on female labour, such as clothing and electronics.

- At a more sociological or anthropological level, it may be worthwhile to further explore how a given "civic culture" develops. Why are citizens in some cities more respectful of laws and more inclined to cooperate than those in other cities? However, this is a "big" question to which there may be no easy answer.

References

Acemoglu, D., S. Johnson and J.A. Robinson (2001). "The Colonial Origins of Comparative Development: An Empirical Investigation," *American Economic Review*, 91 (5): 1369-1401.

Anas, A. and K.S. Lee (1998). *Infrastructure Investment and Productivity: the Case of Nigerian Manufacturing: a Framework for Policy Study.* World Bank, Washington, D.C.

Arsen, David (1997). "Is There Really an Infrastructure/Economic Development Link?" in R. Bingham and R. Mier (eds.), *Dilemmas of Urban Economic Development.* Sage Publications, Thousand Oaks, Calif.: 82-98.

Aschauer, David (1989). "Is Public Expenditure Productive?" *Journal of Monetary Economics*, 23: 177-200.

Aschauer, David (1993). "Genuine Economic Return to Infrastructure Investment," *Policy Studies Journal,* 21 (2): 380-390.

Aschauer, David (2000). "Public Capital and Economic Growth: Issues of Quantity, Finance and Efficiency," *Economic Development and Cultural Change,* 48 (2): 391-406.

Audretsch, D.B. and M.P. Feldman (1996). "R&D Spillovers and the Geography of Innovation and Production," *American Economic Review,* 86 (3): 630-640.

Bairoch, Paul (1988). *Cities and Economic Development: From the Dawn of History to the Present.* University of Chicago Press. Translation of: *De Jéricho à Mexico, villes et économie dans l'histoire,* Gallimard, Paris, 1985.

Bider, S. and T. Smith (1996). "The Linkage between Transportation Infrastructure Investment and Productivity," in Batten D.F. and C. Karlsson (eds.), *Infrastructure and the Complexity of Economic Development.* Springer-Verlaf, Berlin: 49-60.

Bjorvatn, Kjetil (2000). "Urban Infrastructure and Industrialization," *Journal of Urban Economics,* 48: 205-218.

Blaicklock, T. M. (1994). "Financing Infrastructure Projects as Concession," in S. Farrel (ed.), *Financing Transport Infrastructure.* PTRC Education & Research Services, London.

Braczyk, H, P. Cooke and M. Heidenreich (eds.) (1998). *Regional Innovation Systems: The Role of Governance in a Globalized World.* UCL Press, London.

Ciccolla, Pablo (1999). "Globalización y dualización en la región metropolitana de Buenos Aires. Grandes inversiones y reestructuración socioterritorial en los años noventa," *Revista Latinoamericana de Estudios Urbano Regionales,* 25 (76): 5-28.

Ciccone, A. and R.E. Hall (1966). "Productivity and the Density of Economic Activity," *American Economic Review*, 86 (1): 54-70.

Cohen, M. (1996). "The Hypothesis of Urban Convergence" in M. Cohen *et al.*, *Preparing for the Urban Future*. Woodrow Wilson Center Press, Washington, D.C: 25-37.

Crihfield, J.B. and T.J. McGuire (1997). "Infrastructure, Economic Development and Public Policy," *Regional Science and Urban Economics*, 27: 113-116.

De Mattos, Carlos (1999). "Santiago de Chile, globalización y expansión metropolitana: lo que existe sigue existiendo," *Revista Latinoamericana de Estudios Urbano Regionales*, 25 (76): 29-56.

Dumais, G, G. Ellison and E.L. Glaeser (1997). "Geographic Concentration as Dynamic Process", *NBER Working Paper*, No. 6270. On-line at www.nber.org

Duranton, G. and D. Puga (2002). "Diversity and Specialization in Cities: Why, Where and When Does it Matter," in P. McCann (ed.) *Industrial Location Economics*. Edward Elgar, Cheltenham, U.K.

Easterly, W. and R. Levine (2002). "Tropics, Germs, and Crops: How Endowments Influence Economic Development," NBER Working Paper, No. 9106. On-line at www.nber.org

Economist, The (1997). "Russia's Capital: Beacon or Bogey?" *The Economist*, Sept. 6, 1997, London.

Fujita, M. and J.-F. Thisse (2002). *Economics of Agglomeration*. Cambridge. University Press, Cambridge, U.K.

Fukuyama, Francis (1995). *Trust: The Social Virtues and the Creation of Prosperity*. The Free Press, New York.

Gaspar, J. and E. Glaeser (1998). "Information Technology and the Future of Cities," *Journal of Urban Economics*, 43: 136-156.

Gates, L.B. and W.M. Rohe (1987). "Fear and Reactions to Crime: A Revised Model," *Urban Affairs Quarterly*, 22: 425-453.

Gilbert, Alan (ed.) (1996). *The Mega-City in Latin America*. United Nations, University Press, Tokyo.

Glaeser, Edward L. (1998). "Are Cities Dying?" *Journal of Economic Perspectives*, 12 (2): 139-160.

Glaeser, E.L., H.D. Kallal, J.A. Scheinkman and A. Shleifer (1992). "Growth in Cities," *Journal of Political Economy*, 100 (6): 1126- 1152.

Hakfoort, Jacco (1996). "Public Capital, Private Sector Productivity and Economic Growth: A Macro-Economic Perspective," in Batten D.F. and Karlsson, C. (eds.), *Infrastructure and the Complexity of Economic Development*. Springer-Verlaf, Berlin: 61-72.

Hall, Peter (1999). *Cities in Civilization. Culture, Innovation, and Urban Order.* Phoenix Giant, London.

Hall, Peter (2000). "Creative Cities and Economic Development," *Urban Studies*, 37 (4): 639-649.

Heer, Friederich (1962). *The Medieval World* [Chapter 6: Urban Life and Economy]. New American Library, New York & Penguin Books, Markham, Ontario.

Henderson, Vernon (1988). *Urban Development: Theory, Fact and Illusion.* Oxford University Press, New York.

Henderson, Vernon (1997). "Medium Sized Cities," *Regional Science and Urban Economics,* 27: 583-612.

Hoover, Edgar (1948). *The Location of Economic Activity.* McGraw-Hill, New York.

Howe, Frederic (1915) *The Modern City and its Problems.* Charles Scribner's & Sons, New York.

Isard, Walter (1956). *Location and Space Economy.* MIT Press, Cambridge, Mass.

Isard, Walter (1959). *Industrial Complex Analysis and Regional Development.* MIT Press, Cambridge, Mass.

Jacobs, Jane (1969). *The Economy of Cities.* Vintage, New York.

Jacobs, Jane (1984). *Cities and the Wealth of Nations.* Vintage, New York.

Jones, B. and S. Koné (1996). "An Exploration of Relationships between Urbanization and Per Capita Income: United States and Countries of the World," *Papers in Regional Science,* 75 (2): 135-153.

Kessides, Christine (1996). "A Review of Infrastructure's Impact of Economic Development," in D.F. Batten and C. Karlsson (eds.), *Infrastructure and the Complexity of Economic Development.* Springer-Verlaf, Berlin, 213-230.

Kessides, Christine (1992). *The Contributions of Infrastructure to Economic Development: A Review of Experience and Policy Implications.* The World Bank, Washington, D.C.

Krugman, Paul (1991). "Increasing Returns and Economic Geography," *Journal of Political Economy,* 99 (3): 483-499.

Krugman, Paul (1996). "Making Sense of the Competitiveness Debate," *Oxford Review of Economic Policy,* 12: 17-25.

Kuznets, Simon (1968). *Towards a Theory of Economic Growth.* W.W. Norton & Co., New York.

Lall, S., Z. Shalizi and U. Deichmann (2001). *Agglomeration Economies and Productivity in Indian Industry.* Infrastructure and Environment Division, Policy Research Working Paper No. 2663, The World Bank, Washington, D.C.

Landis, David S. (1998). *The Wealth and Poverty of Nations: Why Some are so Rich and Some so Poor.* W.W. Norton & Co., New York and London.

Lee, K.S. (1988). *Infrastructure Constraints on Industrial Growth in Thailand.* Working Paper, Urban Development Division, The World Bank, Washington, D.C.

Lee, K.S. (1989). *Manufacturers' Responses to Infrastructure Deficiencies in Nigeria: Private Alternatives and Policy Options.* The World Bank, Washington, D.C.

Lee, K.S (1992). "Costs of Deficient Infrastructure: The Case of Nigerian Manufacturing," *Urban Studies,* 29 (7): 1071-1092.

Lee, K.S. and A. Anas (1989). *Manufacturers' Responses to Infrastructure Deficiencies in Nigeria: Private Alternatives and Policy Options.* Discussion Paper, Policy, Planning and Research Staff, The World Bank, Washington, D.C.

Lee, K.S., A. Anas and G.-T. Oh (1996). *Costs of Infrastructure Deficiencies in Manufacturing in Indonesia, Nigeria, and Thailand.* Infrastructure and

Energy Division, Policy Research Working Paper No. 1604, The World Bank, Washington, D.C.

Lee, K.S., A. Anas and G.-T. Oh (1999). "Costs of Infrastructure Deficiencies in Manufacturing in Indonesia, Nigeria, and Thailand." *Urban Studies,* 36 (12): 2135-2149.

Lee, K.S, A. Anas, S. Verma and M. Murray (1996). *Infrastructure Bottlenecks, Private Provision and Industrial Productivity.* Infrastructure and Energy Division, Policy Research Working Paper No. 1605, The World Bank, Washington, D.C.

Lemelin, A. and M. Polèse (1995). "What About the Bell-Shaped Relationship Between Primacy and Development?" *International Regional Science Review,* 18: 313-330.

Lobo, J. and N. Rantisi (1999). "Investment in Infrastructure as Determinant of Metropolitan Productivity," *Growth and Change,* 30: 106-127.

Maillat, Denis (1998). *From the Industrial District to the Innovative Milieu: Contribution to an Analysis of Territorialised Production Organizations.* Université de Neuchâtel working paper, Neuchâtel, Switzerland.

Mills, E.S. and B. Hamilton (1994). *Urban Economics* (5th edition). HarperCollins, New York.

Morrison, O.J. and A.E. Schwartz (1992). "State Infrastructure and Productive Performance," *NBER Working Paper,* No. 3981, Washington, D.C.

Munnell, Alicia (1992). "Policy Watch: Infrastructure Investment and Economic Growth," *The Journal of Economic Perspectives,* 6 (4): 189-198.

Nadiri, M.I. and T.P. Mamuneas (1994). "The Effects of Public Infrastructure and R&D Capital on the Cost Structure and Performance of US Manufacturing Industries," *The Review of Economics and Statistics,* 76 (1): 22-37.

OECD (2001). *The Well-being of Nations: The Role of Human and Social Capital.* Organization for Cooperation and Development, Paris.

Olson, Mancur (2000). *Power and Prosperity.* Basic Books, New York.

O'Sullivan, Arthur (2000). *Urban Economics* (4th edition). Irwin McGraw-Hill, Boston.

Parr, John (1999a). "Growth-pole Strategies in Regional Economic Development Planning: A Retrospective View. Part 1. Origins and Advocacy," *Urban Studies,* 36 (7): 1195-1215.

Parr, John (1999b). "Growth-pole Strategies in Regional Economic Development Planning: A Retrospective View. Part 2. Implementation and Outcome," *Urban Studies,* 36 (8): 1247-1268.

Petersen, George et al. (1991). *Urban Economies and National Development.* Office of Housing and Urban Programs, USAID, Washington, D.C.

Pirenne, Henri (1925). *Medieval Cities.* Reprint, Princeton University Press, Princeton.

Polèse, Mario (1994). *Économie urbaine et régionale.* Economica, Paris.

Polèse, Mario (1998a). *Economía urbana y regional: introducción a la relación entre territorio y desarollo.* Asociación de Editoriales Universitarias de América Latina y el Caribe, Libro Universitario Regional, Cartago, Costa Rica.

Polèse, Mario (1998b). *Economia Urbana e Regional.* Colecção APDR, Coimbra, Portugal.

Polèse, Mario (1998c)."Ciudades y empleos en Centroamérica: Elementos para el diseño de estrategias de desarollo económica con base urbana," in M. Lungo and M. Polèse, (eds.), *Economía y desarollo urbana en Centramérica*, FLACSO, San José, Costa Rica.

Polèse, M. and R. Shearmur (2003). "Is Distance Really Dead? Comparing Industrial Location Patterns over Time in Canada," *International Regional Science Review*, forthcoming.

Porter, Michael (1996). "Competitive Advantage, Agglomeration Economies and Regional Policies," *International Regional Science Review*, 19 (1): 85-90.

Porter, Michael (2000). "Location, Competition and Economic Development: Local Clusters in the Global Economy," *Economic Development Quarterly*, 14 (1): 15-34.

PRISMA (1996). *La evolución de la red urbana y el desarollo sostenible en El Salvador.* Programa Salvadoreño de Investigación sobre Desarrollo y Medio Ambiente, San Salvador.

Prud'homme, Rémy (1997). "Urban Transportation and Economic Development," *Région et Développement*, 5: 40-53.

Quigley, John M. (1998). "Urban Diversity and Economic Growth," *Journal of Economic Perspectives*, 12 (2): 127-138.

Rauch, James (1993). "Productivity Gains from Geographic Concentration of Human Capital: Evidence from the Cities," *Journal of Urban Economics*, 34 (3): 380-400.

Reinikka, R. and J. Svensson (1999). *How Inadequate Provision of Public Infrastructure and Services Affects Private Investment.* The World Bank, Washington, D.C.

Rosenthal, S.R. and W.C. Strange (2001). "The Determinants of Agglomeration" *Journal of Urban Economics,* 50: 191-229.

Thomas, C.J. and R. Bromely (2000). "City-Centre Revitalization: Problems of Fragmentation and the Fear in the Evening and Night-Time City," *Urban Studies,* 37 (8): 1403-1429.

Tolley, G.S. and V. Thomas (eds.) (1987). *The Economics of Urbanization and Urban Policies in Developing Nations.* The World Bank, Washington, D.C.

Wang, Eric C. (2002). "Public Infrastructure and Economic Growth: A New Approach Applied to East Asian Economies," *Journal of Policy Modeling,* 5275 : 1-24.

World Bank (1991). *Urban Policy and Economic Development: An Agenda for the 1990's.* The World Bank, Washington, D.C. Spanish title: *Política urbana y desarrollo económico: Un programa para el decenio de 1990.* Banco Mundial (1991).

World Bank (1994). *World Development Report: Infrastructure for Development.* The World Bank, Washington, D.C.

World Bank (1998). *World Development Report; World Development Indicators.* The World Bank, Washington, D.C.

Appendix 1: Survey Questionnaire

AN INTERNATIONAL SURVEY OF THE IMPACT OF LOCAL SERVICES AND INFRASTRUCTURE ON THE OPERATING COSTS OF BUSINESS ESTABLISHMENTS AND ON THEIR CAPACITY TO COMPETE IN GLOBAL MARKETS

UNIVERSIDAD DE COSTA RICA
Escuela de Ingenerio Civil
Programa de Investigación en
Desarollo Urbano Sostenible (PRODUS)

UNIVERSIDAD CENTROAMERICANA
"JOSÉ SIMEÓN CAÑAS"

Université du Québec
Institut national de la recherche scientifique
Urbanisation, Culture et Société

FUNDAÇÃO JOÃO PINHEIRO
Governo de Minas Gerais

INSTITUT NATIONAL DE LA RECHERCHE SCIENTIFIQUE [INRS], MONTRÉAL, QUÉBEC, CANADA

FACULTAD DE ECONOMÍA, UNIVERSIDAD AUTÓNOMA DE PUEBLA, PUEBLA, MÉXICO

ESCOLA DE GOVERNO, FUNDAÇÃO JOÃO PINHEIRO, BELO HORIZONTE, BRASIL

PROGRAMA DE INVESTIGACIÓN EN DESARROLLO URBANA SOSTENIBLE, UNIVERSIDAD DE COSTA RICA, SAN JOSÉ, COSTA RICA

UNIVERSIDAD CENTROAMERICANA "JOSÉ SIMÉON CAÑAS" SAN SALVADOR, EL SALVADOR

With the financial support of the WORLD BANK-NETHERLANDS PARTNERSHIP PROGRAM

Team managers:

Mario Polèse
mario.polese@inrs-ucs.uquebec.ca
(514) 499-4070

Pamela Echeverria
pamela.echeverria@inrs-ucs.uquebec.ca
(514) 499-4050

Date of interview_____   Interviewer Code_____

SUGGESTED RESPONDENTS FOR EACH SECTIONS

SECTION 1   GENERAL INFORMATION REGARDING THE
             ESTABLISHMENT

             Suggested respondent: person in charge of finance or accounting

SECTION 2   TRANSPORT OF GOODS

             Suggested respondent: person in charge of shipping and receiving

SECTION 3   TRANSPORT OF EMPLOYEES

             Suggested respondent: person in charge of personnel and human
             resources

SECTION 4   SAFETY AND SECURITY

             Suggested respondent: person in charge of security

SECTION 5   REGULATORY FRAMEWORK AND URBAN SERVICES

             Suggested respondent: person in charge of governmental relations
             and public administration.

SECTION 6   BUSINESS MEETINGS (1 to 3 questionnaires to be filled out)

             Suggested respondent: executives, managers, or other managerial
             personnel

1. IDENTIFICATION OF CONTACT PERSON (PLEASE ATTACH BUSINESS CARD)

1.1.	Name of respondent	
1.2	Title or position	
1.3.	Telephone number	
1.4.	E-mail	
1.5.	Name of establishment	
1.6.	Type of business	
1.7.	Street address	
1.8.	City	
1.9.	Postal code	

TO BE FILLED OUT BY INTERVIEWER

1. Industry Code (TLC)	2. City Code	3. Location Code

DEFINITIONS

Establishment: This questionnaire refers to your establishment or place of business at a fixed address. If your firm operates several establishments (outlets, warehouses, plants, etc.), the answers in this questionnaire should refer only to the establishment at this address.

Last Reporting Year: The last full year (twelve month period) for which the establishment filed a financial statement or has available financial information. This does not necessarily need to correspond to a calendar year.

Workday: The period (x hours) during which your establishment operates in a typical week. This refers to the operations of your establishment, and not to the work hours of your employees. Thus, a 24-hour workday may comprise three shifts of eight hours.

Workday Lost: A day (or part of day) on which the establishment does not operate at normal capacity. Thus, a day on which the establishment only operates at 50% of its normal level (generating only 50% of its normal output) would be equal to 1/2 a workday lost.

INSTRUCTIONS

- Please answer every question
- If answer has no value, write 0
- If a question does not apply to your establishment, write N/A
- If an answer is unknown or you do not wish to answer, write NSP/PR

SECTION 1: GENERAL INFORMATION
LOCATION AND LEGAL STATUS

1. Which one of the following categories best describes the organisational status of your establishment? *If answer is 1.1 or 1.2, skip question 2*

Organisational status of establishment	Choose one
1.1. Locally-owned establishment, with no affiliates or branches	
1.2. Locally-owned establishment, but linked to a larger organisation or network (by partnerships, franchises, etc.)	
1.3. Branch or subsidiary of a domestically controlled firm or organisation	
1.4. Branch or subsidiary of a foreign controlled firm or organisation	
1.5. Head office of a domestically controlled firm or organisation (with branches or affiliates)	
1.6. Other, please specify:	

2. If your establishment is a branch or subsidiary of a domestically or foreign controlled firm or organisation, please indicate the location of the head office (city and country).

3. In what year did your establishment begin its operation at this address, irrespective of any name changes or changes in ownership?

4. In what type of location does your establishment currently operate?

Type of location	Choose one
3.1. Industrial park or estate	
3.2. Commercial or residential zone	

5. Does your establishment receive any government subsidies or incentives?

1. Yes   What kind
2. No

6. What are the three (3) most important factors that determined the decision to locate your establishment in the Montreal metropolitan area (as opposed to other metropolitan areas)?

Factors	Choose three
6.1. Owner, founder or manager lives (or lived) there	
6.2. Low input costs (raw materials, etc.)	
6.3. Low labour costs	
6.4. Proximity to major clients (centre of your market)	
6.5. Presence of a pool of skilled and educated manpower	
6.6. Proximity to suppliers	
6.7. Presence of complementary firms: repair, technical advice, consulting, etc.	
6.8. Low land or building rental costs	
6.9. Low local taxes	
6.10. Government assistance in establishing your business	
6.11. Favourable business environment	
6.12. Better quality of life	
6.13. Other, please specify:	

CAPITAL STOCK

7. What is the total floor space of this establishment in m² (square meters) or ft² (square feet)?

8. How much did your establishment spend on capital outlays during the last ten years?

Capital outlay	Amount ($) over 10 years
8.1. Land and buildings	
8.2. Machinery, equipment and vehicles	

INPUTS AND OPERATING COSTS

9. What was your establishment's total operating cost, excluding capital outlays?

10. Please breakdown your total operating cost (in %), for the last reporting year, among the following items:

Categories	% of total
10.1. Labour (wages, salaries, fringe and social benefits)	
10.2. Inputs (raw materials, urban services and purchase of external business services)	
10.3. Transportation and communications (transport of goods, communications and travel)	
10.4. Land and buildings	
10.5. Taxes and contributions (local taxes paid to municipality and other contributions to the public sector)	
10.6. Financing costs (dividends, interest, profits, etc.)	
10.7. Other, please specify:	
	100%

11. Please itemize your establishment's three most important raw materials or material inputs and indicate how much was spent on each during the last reporting year?

Raw material or material inputs	Cost ($)
11.1.	
11.2.	
11.3.	

12. Please identify your establishment's most important supplier of inputs or raw materials?

Identification of most important supplier

12.1. Name of establishment	
12.2. Affiliated with your firm?	1. Yes 2. No
12.3. Address	

PRODUCTS AND SALES

13. What was the total value of all goods and services sold by this establishment?

14. What were the three (3) most important products (goods and services) produced at this establishment?

Product or service	Total sales ($)
14.1.	
14.2.	
14.3.	

15. Please distribute your total sales revenue among the following three markets.

Distribution of sales	% of total sales
15.1. Montreal metropolitan area	
15.2. Rest of Canada (outside the metro area)	
15.3. Outside of Canada	
	100%

16. Please identify the principal establishment that is the first destination of your establishment's output.

Identification of chief customer

16.1. Name of establishment	
16.2. Affiliated with your firm?	1. Yes 2. No
16.3. Address	

BUSINESS SERVICES

17. What were the three (3) most important business services (professional services, consultants, etc.) purchased by your establishment?

Business service	Cost ($)
17.1.	
17.2.	
17.3.	

18. Please identify your most important supplier of business services.

Identification of chief business service supplier

18.1. Name of establishment	
18.2. Affiliated with your firm?	1. Yes 2. No
18.3. Address	

EMPLOYMENT

19. How many people worked at this establishment (including owners and managers), on average, during the past 12 months?

    Total employment:

20. Please distribute your workforce by category, and give the following information :

Employment category	Number	% Female	Average monthly wage ($)	University degree (%)
20.1. Managerial and professional				
20.2. Office workers and sales personnel				
20.3. Skilled factory workers				
20.4. Unskilled factory workers				

21. What was the average annual turnover of your workforce during the last five years?

    Note: Average turnover refers to the number of employees, as a percentage of total employees, who left each year and were replaced.

Employment category	Annual rate of turnover (%)
21.1. Managerial and professional	
21.2. Office workers and sales personnel	
21.3. Skilled factory workers	
21.4. Unskilled factory workers	
21.5. Total, if impossible to itemize	

22. How many days are required to train new personnel before they are operational?

Employment category	Days of training
22.1. Managerial and professional	
22.2. Office workers and sales personnel	
22.3. Skilled factory workers	
22.4. Unskilled factory workers	

23. What is the normal number of hours per day, days per week, days per year and weeks per year that your establishment is in operation?

Workdays	Hours, days or weeks
23.1. Hours per work day (maximum=24)	
23.2. Days per week (maximum=7)	
23.3. Weeks per year (maximum=52)	

SECTION 2: TRANSPORTATION OF GOODS

1. Which of the following vehicles does your establishment use to receive or ship merchandise directly to or from your establishment?

Vehicles	Receiving (%)	Shipping (%)
1.1. Large transport trucks		
1.2. Small trucks		
1.3. Other, please specify:		

2. How many of the following vehicles does your establishment own or lease and what was the total associated annual operating cost?

Vehicles	Number of vehicle)	Annual operating cost
2.1. Large transport trucks		
2.2. Small trucks		
2.3. Other, please specify:		

3. If your establishment subcontracts the transport of goods to others, what was the total amount paid to transport companies?

4. On average, what is the frequency of deliveries (arriving at your establishment) and shipments (leaving your establishment)? Indicate the number of trucks coming-in/going-out.

Average frequency of deliveries and shipments Answer the appropriate line	Deliveries (coming in)	Shipments (going out)
4.1. Per day		
4.2. Per week		
4.3. Per month		

5. How often did deliveries arrive late at your establishment during the last 12 months?

Frequency of delivery delays	Choose one
5.1. Never	
5.2. Occasionally (about once a month)	
5.3. Often (about once a week)	
5.4. Frequently (more than once a week)	

6. Do you believe this has affected your establishment's production?

    1. Yes   How, explain
    2. No

7. How often do delays in shipping your products result in the following problems?

Impact of shipping delays	Never	Occasionally (about once a month)	Often (about once a week)	Frequently (more than once a week)
7.1. Customer complaints				
7.2. Loss of customers				
7.3. Incapacity to develop markets where timely delivery is essential				
7.4. Other, please specify:				

8.   Please evaluate the impact of the following factors on the transport costs of your establishment.

Factors impacting transport costs	No Impact	Some Impact	Major Impact
8.1. Poor road conditions and mainte-nance: bad paving, potholes, etc.			
8.2. Traffic congestion			
8.3. Other, please specify:			

9.   With regard to the transport of goods, are there any elements that have not been covered and that you believe have an impact on your establishment? Please specify.

10.   With respect to the transport problems mentioned above (effects of delays, increased vehicle repair and maintenance, etc.), how would you rate their overall impact on the total operating cost of your establishment?

Note: Total operating cost is the value indicated in section 1, question 9.

Impact of transport problems on production costs	Choose one
10.1. Less than 1%	
10.2. 2% - 5%	
10.3. 5% - 7,5%	
10.4. 7,5% - 10%	
10.5. More than 10%	

SECTION 3: TRANSPORTATION OF EMPLOYEES

1.   Please identify the means by which employees commute to and from work?

Transport modes used by the employees of the establishment	% of total
1.1. Public transit (e.g. city bus)	
1.2. Private cars	
1.3. Transport provided by the establishment, including vehicles owned or leased (e.g. bus, minibus)	
1.4. Walk	
1.5. Other, please specify:	
	100%

2.   If employee transportation is provided directly by your establishment or if your establishment reimburses employees for their personal transportation expenses, what was the total amount of compensation paid during the last reporting year?

Total compensation paid ($)	Nature of the compensation (describe)

3.   If your establishment provides employee transportation, what were the reasons for which your establishment chose to provide this service?

Reasons	Choose three
3.1 To prevent late arrival of employees	
3.2. To allow production to continue over longer hours	
3.3. Inadequacy of public transit	
3.4. To ensure the safety of employees	
3.5. Employees live far from the establishment	
3.6. Other, please specify:	

4.   How many parking spaces does your establishment own, rent or otherwise provide for employee use?

5.   How often do employees arrive late for work, causing slowdowns or interruptions to production?

	Choose one
5.1. Less than once a month	
5.2. About once a month	
5.3. About once a week	
5.4. More than once a week	

6.   Please estimate the number of workdays lost due to lateness, in the last 12 months.

7.   With regard to the transport of employees, are there any elements that have not been covered and that you believe have an impact on your establishment? Please specify.

8.   With respect to the problems associated with the transport of employees (effects of absence and lateness, etc.), how would you rate their overall impact on the total operating cost of your establishment?

Note: Total operating cost is the value indicated in section 1, question 9.

Impact of employee transport problems on production cost	Choose one
8.1. Less than 1%	
8.2. 2% - 5%	
8.3. 5% - 7,5%	
8.4. 7,5% - 10%	
8.5. More than 10%	

SECTION 4: SAFETY AND SECURITY

1. Does your establishment have any security installations and equipment?

    1. Yes
    2. No   *Go to question 3*

2. Which of the following security devices does your establishment have and please indicate (below) their total cost?

Safety and security installations	Please check
2.1. Emergency lighting	
2.2. Electric fencing	
2.3. Alarm systems	
2.4. Guard dogs	
2.5. Internal TV circuit	
2.6. Building safety and security equipment or personnel (guardhouses, etc.)	
2.7. Other, please specify:	
2.8. Total Cost	

3. Has your establishment been refused insurance coverage because risks are too high?

    1. Yes
    2. No

    If yes, please specify (afterwards, skip to question 5)

4. What was the annual cost of all insurance premiums paid, related to safety and security considerations (theft, fire, vandalism, personal injury, etc)?

5. How many people are employed by your establishment for security-related work; and what was their total annual wage bill?

Security-related employees (number)	Total annual wage bill ($)

6. If your establishment contracted out any of following security-related services, please check the appropriate answer, also indicating the supplier.

Security services contracted	Who provided the service?		
	Industrial park	A local business association	Private security firms
6.1. Security personnel			
6.2. Security equipment			
6.3. Other, please specify:			
6.4. Total value			

7. Did your establishment contribute in any way (financially or in-kind) to the local police force?

    1. Yes
    2. No

8. How frequently have your establishment, its employees, customers or suppliers, been victims of the following offences during the last 12 months?

Offence	Never	Once a month or less	About once a week	Once a week or more
8.1. Assault with a weapon on the premises				
8.2. Assault with a weapon in the surrounding area (parking lot, street, etc.)				
8.3. Illegal entry and break-ins				
8.4. Vandalism or property damage to grounds, building or equipment				
8.5. Theft of money and embezzlement (from the establishment)				
8.6. Theft of merchandise in the establishment				
8.7. Theft of merchandise being delivered or shipped to your establishment				
8.8. Theft of machines, parts or equipment belonging to the establishment (excluding vehicles)				
8.9. Theft of vehicles (or vehicle parts) belonging to the establishment				
8.10. Theft of vehicles (or vehicle parts) belonging to employees or visitors				
8.11. Theft of personal belonging, including cash, reported by employees or visitors				
8.12. Personal injury to employees, clients, suppliers or visitors, resulting from an offence or criminal behaviour				
8.13. Other, please specify:				

9. What was the approximate cost to your establishment of the following?

Goods or property affected	Cost ($) of loss or damage
9.1. Theft of merchandise	
9.2. Theft (or damage) of equipment, parts or machines	
9.3. Theft (or damage) of vehicles	

10. Please estimate the number of workdays lost during the last 12 months due to theft, vandalism, property damage or personal injury to your employees due to criminal offences?

11. Please identify the factor you believe contributes most to criminal activity in your neighbourhood.

Factors	Choose one
11.1. Inadequate police protection	
11.2. Poor street lighting and visibility	
11.3. Poor design and surveillance of streets and public spaces	
11.4. Neighbourhood that is traditionally violent If so, why?	
11.5. Other, please specify:	

12.   Please rate the safety or your establishment's neighbourhood.

Neighbourhood safety	Choose one
12.1. Very safe	
12.2. Usually safe	
12.3. Unsafe in the evening	
12.4. Rarely or never safe	

13.   Please rate the quality of police protection in your establishment's neighbourhood.

Police protection	Choose one
13.1. Very good	
13.2. Good	
13.3. Average	
13.4. Bad	

14.   Please evaluate how crime or violence affects your establishment, with respect to the following:

Impact of crime and violence	No impact	Minor impact	Significant impact	Major impact
14.1. Ability to keep customers				
14.2. Ability to develop new markets				
14.3. Ability to operate at full capacity (hours during which you can operate)				
14.4. Hiring and retention of female personnel				
14.5. Hiring and retention of male personnel				
14.6. Reliability of your product or service				
14.7. Other, please specify:				

15.   With regard to safety and security, are there elements that have not been covered and that you believe have an impact on your establishment? Please specify.

16.   With respect to the effects of security and safety problems (theft, employee turnover, cost of security services, insurance premiums, etc), how would you rate their overall impact on the total operating cost of your establishment?

Note: Total operating cost is the value given in section 1, question 9.

Impact of security and safety problems on production cost	Choose one
16.1. Less than 1%	
16.2. 2% - 5%	
16.3. 5% - 7.5%	
16.4. 7.5% - 10%	
16.5. More than 10%	

SECTION 5: REGULATORY FRAMEWORK

1. For the following public utilities, what on average is the time required for the service to become operational, from the time of requesting the service to its provision or installation?

Services	Average time required for installation or provision (days, weeks or months)
1.1. Telephones lines (installation and connection)	
1.2. Solid waste collection and disposal (provision)	
1.3. Roads (construction of streets)	
1.4. Electricity (connection and provision)	
1.5. Water (connection)	
1.6. Wastewater treatment (connection)	
1.7. Other, please specify:	

2. Please estimate the number of workdays lost by your establishment in the last 12 months due to failure or delays in the provision of the following service.

Local service failure	Workdays lost
2.1. Telecommunications failures	
2.2. Failures or delays in solid waste collection	
2.3. Power/electricity outages	
2.4. Water shortages or pressures reductions	
2.5. Breakdowns in wastewater treatment	
2.6. Other, please specify:	

3. How much time is required on average to obtain the following local permits (from the time of application to the time of approval) and related costs?

Licences and permits	Average time required for approval (days, weeks or months)	Annual cost ($) of permit
3.1. Business and commercial licenses		
3.2. Building permits		
3.3. Fire code approval		
3.4. Health and safety permits		
3.5. Environmental approval		
3.6. Other, please specify:		

4. When did the following regulatory agencies last inspect your establishment?

Agency / Inspectors	Month and year of last inspection
4.1. Fire inspectors	
4.2. Environmental regulators	
4.3. Health and safety regulators	
4.4. Buildings inspectors	
4.5. Other, please specify:	

5.   For each of the following regulations, please choose the response which best reflects your perception of the appropriateness of standards and approval process.

Procedure	Fire codes	Environ- mental regulations	Health and safety standards	Building codes	Other, please specify
5.1. Appropriateness of standards					
5.1.1. Standards are appropriate; provide sufficient protection for your establishment					
5.1.2. Standards are inappropriate; do not provide adequate protection for your establishment					
5.1.3. Standards are excessive; inhibit your establishment's business					
5.2. Transparency of approval process					
5.2.1. The rules for obtaining approval are easy to understand and fairly administered					
5.2.2. The rules for obtaining approval are unclear and subject to discretion					

6.   What were the three most important factors that determined your establishment's decision to specifically locate at this particular site (rather than another location in the Montreal metropolitan area)?

Features	Choose three
6.1. Proximity to related firms	
6.2. Access to public transportation (for employees)	
6.3. Proximity to customers and markets	
6.4. Proximity to suppliers	
6.5. Access to roads and other transportation infrastructure	
6.6. Access to electricity and power	
6.7. Access to water supplies and services	
6.8. Government assistance or financial aid/tax-free zone	
6.9. Low land and building costs	
6.10. Availability of sufficient floor and ground space	
6.11. Safe neighbourhood	
6.12. Zoning regulations	
6.13. Low municipal taxes	
6.14. Pleasant surroundings	
6.15. Other, please specify:	

7.   If your establishment is considering relocating to another location in the Montreal region, please identify the desired neighbourhood.

8.   How vulnerable is your establishment to unexpected changes in regulations (examples: sudden changes in zoning or regulatory procedures and rules)?

Vulnerability to Administrative Changes	Choose one
8.1. Very vulnerable	
8.2. Somewhat vulnerable	
8.3. Secure	

9.   With regard to the local regulatory framework and public administration, are there any elements that have not been covered and that you believe have an impact on your establishment? Please specify.

10. With respect to the effects of the local regulatory framework and public administration (unreliability of service delivery, discretionary decision making, etc), how would you rate their overall impact on the total operating cost of your establishment?

Note: Total production cost is the value indicated in section 1, question 9.

Impact of local regulatory framework and public administration on total production cost	Choose one
10.1. Less than 1%	
10.2. 2% - 5%	
10.3. 5% - 7,5%	
10.4. 7,5% - 10%	
10.5. More than 10%	

SECTION 6: BUSINESS MEETINGS

Note to respondents
Three (3) copies of this part of the questionnaire have been provided. At least one copy should be filed out (maximum of three). We recommend that this part of the questionnaire be filled out by executives of your establishment or other persons in high-level positions: plant manager, executive officers, etc.

1.   How important is it for you to meet at least once a month with the following persons?

Persons to meet with	Very important	Important	Not important
1.1. Clients: current or potential			
1.2. Suppliers of goods and services, including repair and maintenance			
1.3. Consultants: technical, legal, marketing, etc.			
1.4. Bankers, financial advisors, insurance agents, pension fund managers, etc.			
1.5. Competitors, business partners and other business acquaintances			
1.6. Political or administrative representatives			
1.7. Other, please specify:			

2.   How many days per month do you spend away from your office, on average, on business travel outside of the Montreal metropolitan area?

3. How many local business meetings do you attend on average per week in the Montreal metropolitan area, and how many hours do these meetings generally take?

Note: A local business meeting is a meeting that takes place in the Montreal metro area, but outside your establishment.

Average number of meetings per week	Hours per meeting

4. What transport mode do you generally use to go to and from local business meetings?

Transport mode for local business meetings	% of Total
4.1. Automobile	
4.2. Other, please specify:	
	100%

5. How often did you miss local business meetings because of road and traffic conditions in the last 12 months?

Frequency of meetings missed	Choose one
5.1. Never	
5.2. About once a month	
5.3. About once a week	
5.4. More than once a week	

6. Please evaluate to what extend meetings missed or forgone have had the following impacts on your establishment in the last 12 months:

Impact of missed or foregone business meetings	Significant	Moderate	None or very little
6.1. Prevented timely repairs, slowing down or halting production			
6.2. Opportunities lost: potential clients not met, resulting in fewer customers and lower market share			
6.3. Information lost: informants or consultants not met, resulting in being less up-to-date on the latest innovations and market opportunities			
6.4. Value of time lost on travel			
6.5. Other, please specify:			

7. How would you evaluate the impact of business meetings missed or foregone on your establishment's productivity?

Impact	Choose one
7.1. Major Impact	
7.2. Some Impact	
7.3. No or Little Impact	

8. With regard to business meetings, are there any elements that have not been covered and that you believe have an impact on your establishment? Please specify.

Appendix 2:
Template of Focus Groups

Grupo de trabajo sobre los servicios locales en la industria textil y vestuario/ industria alimenticia

El impacto de los servicios locales sobre los costos de operación de las empresas

Université du Québec
Institut national de la recherche scientifique
Urbanisation, Culture et Société

Apertura

- Palabras de bienvenida (3 minutos)
    - Presentación de la animadora y asistente de relatoria
    - Presentación de participantes y explicación del funcionamiento del grupo de trabajo

- Propósito del encuentro (3 minutos)
    - Deseamos conocer el impacto de la calidad de los servicios locales sobre el funcionamiento de las empresas

    En qué medida la deficiencia de los servicios provocan gastos adicionales (o genera perdidas)

Université du Québec
Institut national de la recherche scientifique
Urbanisation, Culture et Société

Misión de los participantes

- Esta reunión es un complemento de la primera fase del proyecto (aplicación de un cuestionario en su empresa).
    - La mesa redonda concierne exclusivamente a los gastos de funcionamiento de las empresas

- Esperamos obtener de ustedes información que nos permita complementar las respuestas obtenidas de la encuesta aplicada

Université du Québec
Institut national de la recherche scientifique
Urbanisation, Culture et Société

Método y programa

- Presentación de los cinco servicios (3 minutos)

- El estudio de cada uno de los servicios (100 minutos)
    - *Esta previsto dedicar más tiempo al primer servicio, de manera que los participantes se familiarizen con nuestro método*

- Conclusiones (5 minutos)

Université du Québec
Institut national de la recherche scientifique
Urbanisation, Culture et Société

Los cinco servicios

Transporte de mercancías (30 minutos)

Transporte de personas:
empleados y administradores

Seguridad y protección

Servicios urbanos

Aplicación de regulaciones

70 minutos

Université du Québec
Institut national de la recherche scientifique
Urbanisation, Culture et Société

Estudio del primer servicio: *transporte de mercancías*

Université du Québec
Institut national de la recherche scientifique
Urbanisation, Culture et Société

Transporte de mercancías (3 minutos)

Calidad de la red vial, control del tráfico de vehículos y seguridad vial

Servicios	Ejemplos de costos y medidas paliativas
• Escasez de infraestructura y red vial incompleta o carente mantenimiento • Control del tráfico y seguridad vial	• Atrasos: impacto sobre el progreso de la producción y sobre los servicios a los usuarios • Aumento de los gastos de reparación de los vehículos • Aumento del consumo de combustible debido a la congestión y a las condiciones viales • Aumento de las primas de seguro de los vehículos • Bienes dañados o destruídos debido a la mala calidad vial • Gastos « invisibles » asumidos por el personal (chóferes, mecánicos)
	• **Los repartos son hechos de noche o temprano por la mañana para evitar la congestión; compra de vehículos más resistentes**

Université du Québec
Institut national de la recherche scientifique
Urbanisation, Culture et Société

Transporte de mercancías
Tareas del grupo de trabajo

- Identificación de los principales factores que afectan los gastos

(8-12 minutos)

Université du Québec
Institut national de la recherche scientifique
Urbanisation, Culture et Société

Transporte de mercancías
Tareas del grupo de trabajo

- Estimación de los gastos relacionados a los problemas de transporte de mercancías

Estimación en % del costo total

   – Búsqueda de un acuerdo general

(8-12 minutos)

Université du Québec
Institut national de la recherche scientifique
Urbanisation, Culture et Société

Estudio del segundo servicio:
transporte de personas
(empleados y administradores)

Université du Québec
Institut national de la recherche scientifique
Urbanisation, Culture et Société

Transporte de personas (2 minutos)

Facilidad de los movimientos dentro de la ciudad, control del tráfico de vehículos, seguridad vial y transporte público

Servicios	Ejemplos de costos y medidas paliativas
• Sistema de transporte público • Escasez de infraestructura y red vial incompleta o carente mantenimiento • Control del tráfico y seguridad vial • Estacionamiento	• Retrasos de los empleados: tiempo de trabajo perdido; estrés y fatiga de los empleados; efectos negativos sobre la productividad • Para viajes de negocios: tiempo perdido; reducción de las reuniones con los clientes; impacto sobre la eficacia del trabajo de los administradores; información perdida
	• **La empresa suministra el transporte a los empleados; debe ajustar los horarios de trabajo (horas); los administradores evitan hacer más de una reunión por día (fuera de la oficina)**

Université du Québec
Institut national de la recherche scientifique
Urbanisation, Culture et Société

Transporte de personas

Tareas del grupo de trabajo

• Identificación de los principales factores que afectan a los gastos

(5-8 minutos)

Université du Québec
Institut national de la recherche scientifique
Urbanisation, Culture et Société

Transporte de personas

Tareas del grupo de trabajo

- Estimación de los gastos relacionados a los problemas de transporte de personas

Estimación en % del costo total

– Búsqueda de un acuerdo general

(7-10 minutos)

Université du Québec
Institut national de la recherche scientifique
Urbanisation, Culture et Société

Estudio del tercer servicio:
seguridad y protección

Université du Québec
Institut national de la recherche scientifique
Urbanisation, Culture et Société

Seguridad y protección (2 minutos)

Calidad de los servicios políciacos y otros servicios públicos que garantizan la seguridad en los distritos comerciales

Servicios	Ejemplos de costos y medidas paliativas
• Protección policíaca • Alumbrado público y sistemas de vigilancia • Servicio público de protección contra los incendios	• Robo o daño a los bienes y a los equipos; lesiones corporales a los empleados y a los clientes; primas de seguros altas; gastos de servicios de protección privados • Tiempo de producción perdido o número de ocasiones que ha perdido negocios debido a bienes robados o dañados • Dificultad en conservar o contratar empleados; dificultad o imposibilidad de tener jornádas (cuartos) de trabajo por la tarde
	• **La empresa solicita servicios de protección privados o compra de equipo de protección; realiza contribuciones a la fuerza policiaca**

Université du Québec
Institut national de la recherche scientifique
Urbanisation, Culture et Société

Seguridad y protección

Tareas del grupo de trabajo

- Identificación de los principales factores que afectan los gastos

(5-8 minutos)

Université du Québec
Institut national de la recherche scientifique
Urbanisation, Culture et Société

Seguridad y protección

Tareas del grupo de trabajo

- Estimación de los gastos relacionados a los problemas de seguridad y protección

Estimación en % del costo total

– Búsqueda de un acuerdo general

(7-10 minutos)

Université du Québec
Institut national de la recherche scientifique
Urbanisation, Culture et Société

Estudio del cuarto servicio:

servicios urbanos

Université du Québec
Institut national de la recherche scientifique
Urbanisation, Culture et Société

Servicios urbanos (1 minuto)
Eficacia general de los servicios

Servicios	Ejemplos de costos y medidas paliativas
• Agua y drenaje; recolección de desechos sólidos y disposición de basura	• Espera para la conexión a los servicios (p.ej.: agua); riesgo de salud para los empleados • Interrupción del servicio; frecuencia de la recolección de basura (insuficiente)

Université du Québec
Institut national de la recherche scientifique
Urbanisation, Culture et Société

Servicios urbanos
Tareas del grupo de trabajo

• Identificación de los principales factores que afectan los gastos

(2-4 minutos)

Université du Québec
Institut national de la recherche scientifique
Urbanisation, Culture et Société

Servicios urbanos

Tareas del grupo de trabajo

- Estimación de los gastos relacionados a los servicios urbanos

Estimación en % del costo total

— Búsqueda de un acuerdo general

(4-5 minutos)

Université du Québec
Institut national de la recherche scientifique
Urbanisation, Culture et Société

Estudio del quinto servicio:
aplicación de las regulaciones

Université du Québec
Institut national de la recherche scientifique
Urbanisation, Culture et Société

Aplicación de las regulaciones (1 minuto)

Licencias, regulaciones de zonas, códigos de construcción, etc

Servicios	Ejemplos de costos y medidas paliativas

• Administración de las regulaciones locales sobre el uso del suelo
• Permisos de inspección (incendio, construcción, equipos sanitarios)
	• Tiempo y producción perdido; espera para licencias;
	  tiempo perdido en las negociaciones
	• Zonificación, regulaciones y permisos: incertidumbre
	  del uso del suelo; decisiones arbitrarias; impacto negativo sobre la planeación y la inversión

	• La empresa contrata personal para realizar los procedimientos administrativos; se proporcionan ciertos servicios (ej: agua, equipamiento sanitario); contribuye monetariamente o de otra forma a las autoridades o a los administradores públicos

Université du Québec
Institut national de la recherche scientifique
Urbanisation, Culture et Société

Aplicación de las regulaciones
Tareas del grupo de trabajo

• Identificación de los principales factores que afectan los gastos

(2-4 minutos)

Université du Québec
Institut national de la recherche scientifique
Urbanisation, Culture et Société

Aplicación de las regulaciones

Tareas del grupo de trabajo

- Estimación de los gastos relacionados a la applicacion de regulaciones

Estimación en % del costo total

   — Búsqueda de un acuerdo general

(4-5 minutos)

Université du Québec
Institut national de la recherche scientifique
Urbanisation, Culture et Société

Conclusión

Cuadro síntesis

(5 minutos)

Université du Québec
Institut national de la recherche scientifique
Urbanisation, Culture et Société

Cuadro de síntesis y reiteración
Costos atribuibles al mal funcionamiento de los servicios

Servicios	Estimación en % del costo total de funcionamiento	± % *
Transporte de mercancías		
Transporte de personas		
Seguridad y protección		
Servicios urbanos		
Aplicación de las regulaciones		

Si no se llega a un acuerdo, indicar un porcentaje en un rango mas o menos

Université du Québec
Institut national de la recherche scientifique
Urbanisation, Culture et Société

Agradecimiento a los participantes

Université du Québec
Institut national de la recherche scientifique
Urbanisation, Culture et Société

AGMV Marquis

MEMBER OF SCABRINI MEDIA

Quebec, Canada
2003